Hats On!

Hats On!

31 Warm and Winsome Caps for Knitters

By Charlene Schurch

Color photographs by Lynn Karlin
Drawings by Marie Litterer

Down East Books

CAMDEN, MAINE

To my mother, Anne Tompkins, who taught me so many things,
including how to knit, in such an expansive way that it made the books possible.

Copyright © 1999 by Charlene Tompkins Schurch
ISBN 0-89272-435-8
Library of Congress Catalog Card Number: 99-72212
Book design by Janet L. Patterson
Printed at Bookcrafters, Inc.

5   4   3

Down East Books / Camden, Maine
Orders: (800) 766-1670

CONTENTS

INTRODUCTION

The knitted cap has been with us in one form or another for a long time, some historians think even longer than the knitted sock, though in searching for information about head gear I found far more about "fashionable" styles worn by wealthy people (who invariably wore felted models) than about the more practical caps of the common folk, which were hand-knitted pieces.

The knitted caps or other cloth caps worn by laborers or peasants were day-to-day clothing and were not saved. But once in a while we are given a fortunate glimpse at what people wore centuries ago. The *Mary Rose*, Henry VIII's warship, sank in the late sixteenth century and was raised recently. It provided a wealth of artifacts from that time, including knitted caps. They are tam-shaped on top, with a brim, and look like they were fulled after knitting. The shape is very similar to the French beret and the Scottish tam.

Another early example of knitted caps are the Monmouth caps, which are circular and hug the head. They were considered so indispensable that they were listed by name by the London Company for colonists to bring when moving to the Massachusetts Bay Colony. German peasants wore white caps with slightly longer bodies and pointed crowns that look like the "sleep caps" of Victorian times. A cap of this basic shape was also popular in Estonia.

Our current view of the knitted cap is still influenced by the early twentieth century emergence of outdoor sports for the upper classes, specifically skiing in the Alps and ice-skating. A "proper" felted cap would probably not stay on the head or keep the athlete as warm as does a "close-fitting knitted turban."

I am a fan of small knitting projects, notably caps; they are portable, quick to make, a good way to try a new pattern or technique, and are often the right size for a gift to a relative or neighbor. Many times you can knit a cap from yarn in your stash without having to invest in more yarn (my apologies to yarn sellers everywhere). Lastly, caps are a wonderful and generous gift to a charity, be it a homeless or battered women's shelter, or many of the other such groups. It is satisfying and helps many people stay warmer.

The caps in this collection of patterns are contemporary, though many have a traditional look. They are beautiful and timeless—the Scandinavian patterns along with the Aran styles will no doubt be popular for years to come. Most patterns are written in four sizes—two for children and two for adults—but in some cases the specifics of the pattern made it excessively difficult to design in all the sizes. When dealing with a pattern repeat of thirty stitches, spanning the size range is difficult, if not impossible. But remember that caps stretch, and by altering the yarn and/or needle size and knitting a test swatch you should be able to achieve a specific size.

To select the proper size, measure the wearer's head around the ears and subtract two to four inches. It is not always safe to decide that someone will wear a size based on age or height; some youngsters have large heads and some tall, quite large people have small heads. But be encouraged—caps are elastic and fit a wide range.

My intent was to create a book that you can use for the whole family for a long time. The last few caps in the book are a testament to whimsy—while watching the Olympics and other skiing events on television I saw a good number of "fun" caps. No reason to deprive the hand knitter of such entertaining projects.

There are many techniques here, from plain stockinette caps, to single-color pattern, to multicolor-stranded knitting, and some fun shapes that I hope will cheer you as you knit, and then see them worn in cool weather. I trust that you will find many styles that please and challenge you.

I want to express my sincere gratitude to all the published knitters who have provided untold information and inspirations. Particular thanks go to those who kept encouraging me when it seemed no one wanted this book: Susan Guagliumi, Beth Brown-Reinsel, and Meg Swansen.

Thanks also go to my husband, Fred, who cajoles, encourages, listens, and makes an enormous contribution to my life every day.

— C. S.

TECHNIQUES

CASTING ON

The cast-on is important to any garment, but especially to a cap. Almost all of the caps in this book are started at the cuff and worked to the crown, so the cast-on edge is visible around the forehead of the wearer. A beautiful cast-on will disappear (sad to say), and a less than perfect (too tight, or loose and rippling) cast-on may become the one thing you can't take your eyes off.

I have recommended several cast-ons; depending on the design of the cap, different cast-ons are appropriate. There are many names given to ways to cast on, which can be confusing—it confused me also for a while. I have standardized my terminology and am using names established by Montse Stanley in *The Handknitter's Handbook.*

Chain Cast-On

Make a slip knot and place it on the left needle. Insert right needle into the loop, knit a stitch and place it on the left needle, turned. Continue knitting as shown in Photo 1, working through the last stitch.

This method produces a very loose cast-on that at the base of a cap would be unsatisfactory; however, it is flexible and makes it easy to pick up the stitches for a secure hem.

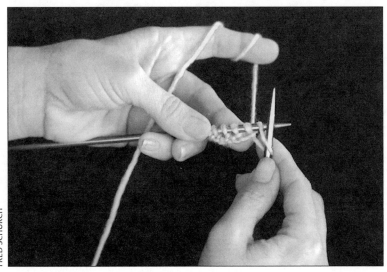

PHOTO 1.
Chain Cast-On.

Two-Strand Cast-On

Make a slip knot with a tail about four times the length of the cap circumference (e.g., for a 20-inch cap leave an 80-inch tail). We will refer to the *tail*—the free end, and the *long end*—the yarn attached to the ball of yarn. Insert needle into the slip knot. Both lengths of yarn are held in the left hand, the tail over the thumb, and the long end over the index finger. Both ends are tensioned by holding them in the palm with the other fingers (Photo 2). The needle, which is held in the right hand, is inserted into the front of the loop on the thumb (Photo 3) and laid on top of the yarn on the index finger. This yarn is dipped down by the needle and pulled through the loop on the thumb (Photo 4), forming a loop on the

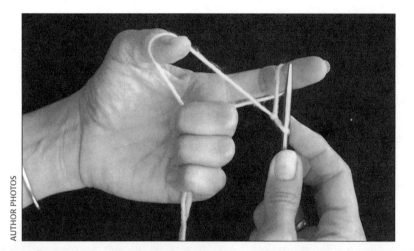

PHOTO 2.
Beginning the Two-Strand Cast-On.

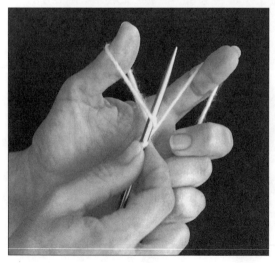

PHOTO 3.
Inserting needle through thumb loop.

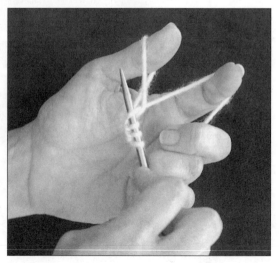

PHOTO 4.
Pulling the strand through.

needle that is adjusted by placing the thumb under the yarn now coming from the needle and gently pulling back on it, this same motion setting up the loop on the thumb for the next stitch. Repeat this operation for the required number of stitches.

Two-Strand Cast-On Using Two Colors

Use the Two-Strand Cast-on method. Make a slip knot about three inches from the end of both balls of yarn. Place both on the needle. (These slip knots will be removed from the needle before you begin knitting the first round.) Now cast on as for the Two-Strand Cast-on above, with one color over the thumb and the other over the index finger (Photo 5). Repeat until you have the correct number of stitches, not counting the two slip knots, which will be taken off the needle after all the casting on is complete.

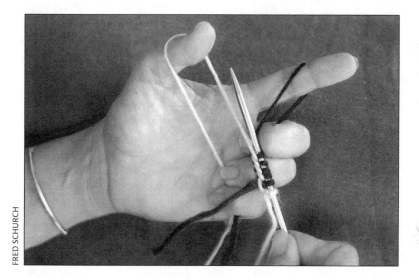

PHOTO 5.
*Two-Strand
Cast-On using
two colors.*

FRED SCHURCH

Two-Strand Cast-On for Knit-and-Purl Ribbing

Make a slip knot for the initial stitch at a distance from the end of the yarn of about 4 times the distance needed for the ribbing. Since the first slip knot will look like a knit stitch, we will start with a purl stitch cast-on and then work alternately, knit 1 and purl 1, ending with a purl stitch. (In the round, k1, p1 ribbing requires an even number of stitches; k2, p2 ribbing requires a number of stitches divisible evenly by 4.)

Hold the needle in your right hand with the tail hanging forward and the ball end behind. Insert your left thumb and index finger between the two strands, spread them apart, and grab the strands with the last three fingers of your left hand slightly. What is happening with this cast-on is that the loop on the thumb is like a stitch on the left-hand needle and the yarn around the index finger is like the yarn on the continental knitter's left finger when knitting. The motion of the needle and yarn is the same, and you get alternate knit and purl stitches as you will when ribbing.

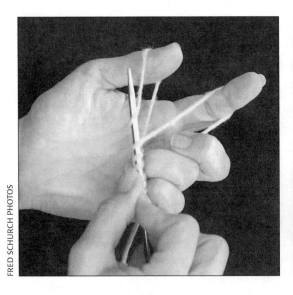

PHOTO 6.
Bringing needle behind front strands of both loops.

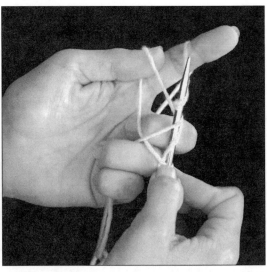

PHOTO 7.
Catching the index-finger loop.

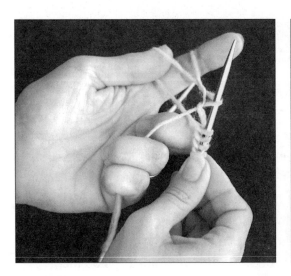

PHOTO 8.
Drawing new stitch back through thumb loop.

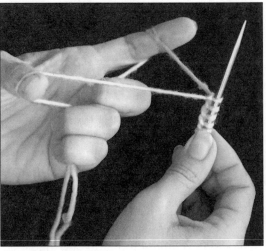

PHOTO 9.
Completed purl cast-on.

Purl: Bring the needle behind front strand of index finger loop, then behind front strand of thumb loop (Photo 6), up and over front strand of index loop (Photo 7), catching it and backing it out under the front of the thumb loop (Photo 8). One purl stitch cast on (Photo 9).

Knit: Bring needle under front strand of thumb loop, up over front strand of index loop, catch it and bring it under the front of the thumb loop, and use it to adjust tension on the new stitch. One knit stitch cast on.

Continue working purl cast-on, knit cast-on until you have the correct number of stitches.

Yarn-Over Tubular Cast-On

With slippery yarn, such as cotton, and a large crochet hook, make a chain of the number of stitches you want to cast on, and then cut the yarn and run the end through the last stitch so it won't unravel. With the cap yarn and knitting needle, make a slip knot and pick it up through the loop (bump) on the back of the chain, *yarn over, skip one chain bump, and pick up a stitch through the next crochet stitch bump.* (Photos 10 and 11.) Continue around until you have the number of stitches needed for the cap. You will have an even number, ending with a yarn-over. Place marker.

Carefully arrange the stitches so they are not twisted and begin working.

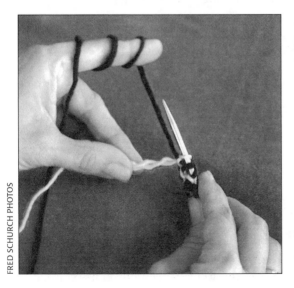

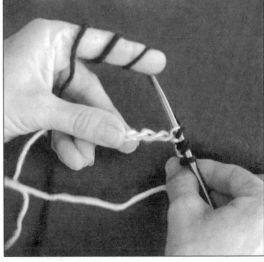

PHOTO 10.
Inserting needle through chain.

PHOTO 11.
Picking up the index-finger strand.

Round 1A: *Slip one with yarn in back, p1*; continue to work around.

Round 1B: *K1, slip one with yarn in front*; continue to work around. (This is what is known as double knitting in some circles, and you have just worked one complete round.)

Round 2A: Repeat Round 1A.

Round 2B: Repeat Round 1B.

Round 3: Begin working ribbing in normal manner: k1, p1.

Once you have finished the cap, unravel the crochet chain.

USING CIRCULAR AND DOUBLE-POINTED NEEDLES

One of the big advantages of knitting in the round is that when the knitting is completed you are just about finished with the project—there is no sewing together. One thing you have to be very careful about in the first round of knitting is that the stitches are not twisted, as this will create a Möbius Strip, which is interesting but not the shape we are looking for in a cap. If you find that you have not aligned all the stitches to the same direction, you have one chance to rescue the situation before starting over. At the beginning of the round, before you start knitting the second round, you can twist the whole thing straight, being careful that you don't drop a stitch, but this little bit of care is better than beginning again.

With most of the caps here you will be required to switch to double-pointed needles at some point, as the fabric will be too small to fit around the 16-inch circular needle. You can wait until the working gets difficult and then make the transition, or you may make the change when you begin working the crown decreases, which is the method I prefer. I try to arrange the stitches in segments so that all the stitches being decreased are on the same double-pointed needle. That is, for a cap with four crown segments I use five double-pointed needles, one for each segment and one to work. I never have to knit two together from two different needles that way.

TASSELS

Make tassels by winding yarn 40 times around a 4-inch piece of cardboard. (I like to use a half-inch stack of 4″ x 6″ note cards, as they are stiffer than a piece of cardboard and require no measuring or cutting.) Take six strands of yarn 24 inches long (four strands if you are going to make a Lanyard Braid). Place the strands through the yarn wound on the cardboard. Pull so that the ends are even. Slide the cards out of the tassel. Secure the end of the tassel about ¾ inch from where the braid is attached by taking a piece of yarn and winding it around the tassel three times tightly. Cut the ends of the tassel. Now make the cord of your choice.

POM-POMS

Cut a piece of heavy cardboard as wide as you want the diameter of the pom-pom to be. Wrap yarn 40 to 50 times around cardboard. Slip the loops off the cardboard, tie tightly in the center, and cut loops. Shake the pom-pom to fluff it out, and trim evenly.

BRAID AND CORDS

It is best to work a few more inches of cord than you think you'll need.

Twisted Cord

Cut several strands of yarn, three times the desired length of the finished cord. Knot both ends, keeping the ends at even tension. Hook or pin one end and insert a pencil through the other. Turn pencil over and over, until the strands are well twisted. Fold in half, keeping the cord taut to avoid tangling. Knot the two ends together, let the cord twist back on itself, and even out the turns.

Finger Crochet Cord

Work from two balls of yarn. Make a slip knot in the end of each strand.

1. Place the slip knot from the right hand through the slip knot in the left hand; snug up the slip knot in the left-hand color.

2. Draw the left strand through the right loop. Hold this loop over the left index finger and tighten the right loop with the right hand. (Photo 12, next page.)

3. Draw the right strand through the left-hand loop. Hold this loop over the right index finger and tighten the left loop with the left hand.

4. Repeat steps 2 and 3 alternately until you have the length of cord you need.

Lanyard Braid

This is the same technique many have learned at summer camp using plastic lacing. Using two colors is fun—if both strands of one color are on the same side, you get a diamond pattern, while if you have a light and dark on each side there will be a spiral. You also have the option of using solid color.

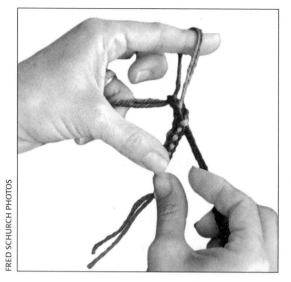

PHOTO 12.
Finger crochet. Drawing the left strand through.

PHOTO 13.
Adding a lanyard braid to a tassel.

1. Lanyard braid uses four strands of yarn. I use a double thickness of yarn for each "strand." Take four equal lengths of yarn and slip through the end of the tassel. Even up the ends. Arrange the lengths of yarn into four double-thickness strands. Fan out the strands slightly. The strand farthest to the left is in position #1. Positions #2 and #3 are in the middle, and position #4 is farthest to the right.

2. Start with the strand in position #4, bringing that strand to the left and behind the two center strands, then in front of the #2 strand, ending at position #3. (The strand that started out in #4 position is now in the #3 position, and the former #3 strand is now in the #4 position.)

3. Now take the strand in the #1 position and bring it behind the two center strands, then in front of the #3 strand, ending in the #2 position. (Photo 13.)

Continue working in this order until you have the length you desire.

Attaching the Cord to the Cap

The cord needs to be threaded into the hole at the top of the cap. This is easiest to do by carefully taking the strands you are working with and slipping them into the cap from the outside. Pull the cord inside and tie a knot in the cord large enough to prevent the it from pulling out. Trim the ends. If this cap is to be worn by a child and you fear that it may be grabbed by the tassel, you may want to sew the knot to the top of the cap on the inside.

Turkish-Patterned Cap (page 58), Fana Cap (page 46), and Topflappen Cap (page 80).

Crown detail of Topflappen Cap.

Crown detail of Turkish-Patterned Cap.

Triple-Patterned Watch Cap (page 34), Cap with Slip-Stitch Cable (page 60), and Aran Watch Cap (page 30).

Crown detail of Triple-Patterned Watch Cap.

Norwegian Star (page 42), Striped Watch Cap with Pointed Crown (page 27), and Tam (page 65).

Cap with Turk's Head Cuff (page 64), Bohus-Patterned Cap (page 62), and Tassled Fez (page 56).

Brimmed Cap (page 79), Gansey Watch Cap (page 36), and Doublemaasa Cap (page 38).

Left to right: Stockinette Watch Cap (page 26), Fair Isle Cap (page 54),
Classic Watch Cap (page 25).

Lace Rib Watch Cap (page 28),
Komi Cap (page 44), and
Lusekofte Cap (page 51).

Clockwise from left: Rolled-Cuff
Cap with Star Crown (page 67),
Andean Cap with Earflaps
(page 68), and Child's Andean
Cap (page 70).

Clockwise from upper left: Lusekofte Cap (page 51) with Optional X-Pattern, Danish Earflap Cap (page 72), Ullared Cap (page 48), and All-Over Two-Color Patterned Watch Cap (page 32).

Crown detail of Danish Earflap Cap.

Crown detail of All-Over Two-Color Patterned Watch Cap.

Crown detail of Ullared Cap.

Jester's Cap (page 76) and Multicolor Whimsical Cap (page 74).

Two-Color Christmas Ornament (page 85) and Bavarian Tree Ornament (page 83).

Classic Watch Cap

The design of this cap is based on the "official" Watch Cap worn by Navy personnel. It is modest in its elegance and simple to knit. (Pictured on page 20.)

INSTRUCTIONS

With circular needle cast on 112 (128, 144, 160) stitches using Yarn-Over Tubular Cast-On (page 13). Join, being careful not to twist.

Body: Work k1, p1 ribbing for 9 (10, 11, 12) inches. Work one more round in ribbing, placing 28 (32, 36, 40) stitches on each of the four double-pointed needles, and beginning each needle with a purl stitch.

Crown: Work decrease round as follows: *P1, k1, p1, ssk, work in established rib until 2 stitches remain on the needle, k2 tog*. Repeat around and continue this pattern repeat until there are 6 stitches on each needle.

> Next to final round: *P1, k1, p1, sl1, k2 tog, psso*; repeat around.
> Final round: *sl1, k2 tog, psso, k1*; repeat around.

Break off the yarn with a tail about 8 inches long and thread the end into a yarn needle. Draw the thread through remaining stitches and fasten off.

For information on converting measurements and yarn weights to metric, see page 88.

SIZES: Small (Medium, Large, X-Large). Cap circumference as worn 16 (18, 20, 22) inches; unstretched circumference 11.2 (12.8, 14.4, 16) inches.

YARN: Sport weight, 184 yds per 1¾ oz; 1 (2, 2, 2) skeins.

GAUGE: 10 stitches = 1 inch over k1, p1 rib.*

NEEDLES: Circular needle, 16-in length, and one set of dpn, both size 4, or size needed to knit to gauge. *(For equivalent Canadian/ British and metric needle sizes, see page 88.)*

*To make a gauge swatch, cast on 40 stitches with your cap yarn and needles. Work k1, p1 rib back and forth for 3 inches. Measure the swatch on a flat surface. My gauge: 40 stitches = 4 inches unstretched.

Stockinette Watch Cap

This is a simple-to-knit cap with a warm double-ribbed cuff.
(Pictured on page 20.)

For information on converting measurements and yarn weights to metric, see page 88.

SIZES: Small (Medium, Large, X-Large). Cap circumference 16 (18, 20, 22) inches.

YARN: Worsted weight, 100% wool, 4-ply, 210 to 220 yds per 3½ oz; 1 skein.

GAUGE: 5½ stitches = 1 inch over stockinette stitch knit in the round.

NEEDLES: Circular needle, 16-in length, and one set of dpn, both size 6, or size needed to knit to gauge.
(For equivalent Canadian/ British and metric needle sizes, see page 88.)

INSTRUCTIONS

With circular needle cast on 88 (100, 110, 120) stitches using Yarn-Over Tubular Cast-On (page 13). Join, being careful not to twist.

Cuff: Work k1, p1 ribbing for 4 (4½, 5½, 6) inches.

Body: Work stockinette stitch for 2¾ (3½, 3½, 4) inches. In the final round of the body some of the sizes need to have their total stitch count amended for the crown: 0, (-1, 0, +1). Total stitches on needle: 88, (99, 110, 121).

Crown: Switch to double-pointed needles now, or when there are too few stitches to support the circular needle. Decrease 11 stitches every other round.

Round 1: *K6 (7, 8, 9), k2 tog, place marker*; repeat around.

Round 2 and all even-numbered rounds: Knit around.

Round 3 and remaining odd-numbered rounds: *K to 2 stitches before a marker, k2 tog*; repeat around.

Once finished, break off the yarn with an 8-inch tail and thread the end into a yarn needle. Draw the thread through remaining stitches and fasten off.

Striped Watch Cap with Pointed Crown

This cap has a longer crown than the other watch caps and is decorated with a jaunty tassel and cord. You can work it in a single color or in stripes—one of the easiest ways to introduce multiple colors in knitting. I've used a Fibonacci sequence of 2, 3, 5, 8, 5, 3 rounds for each color. The Fibonacci sequences produce very pleasing combinations. (Pictured on page 19.)

INSTRUCTIONS

With circular needle cast on 88 (100, 112, 120) stitches using Yarn-Over Tubular Cast-On (page 13). Join, being careful not to twist.

Cuff: Work k1, p1 ribbing for 4 (4½, 5½, 6) inches. Knit one round plain.

Crown: Switch to double-pointed needles now, or when there are too few stitches to support the circular needle.

>   Round 1: *K20 (22, 26, 28), k2 tog, place marker*; repeat around.
>   Rounds 2, 3, and 4: knit around.
>   Round 5 and every fourth round thereafter; *k to 2 stitches before a marker, k2 tog*; repeat around. The intervening 3 rounds are worked plain around.

Continue until there are 4 stitches left. Break off the yarn with about an 8-inch tail and thread the end into a yarn needle. Draw the thread through remaining stitches and fasten off.

Tassel and cord: Make a tassel (see page 14) and attach it to the cap with a lanyard braid (page 15).

For information on converting measurements and yarn weights to metric, see page 88.

SIZES: Small (Medium, Large, X-Large). Cap circumference 16 (18, 20, 22) inches.

YARN: Worsted weight, 100% wool, 4-ply, 210 to 220 yds per 3½ oz; 1 skein per color, 6 to 8 oz total weight.

GAUGE: 5½ stitches and 8 rounds = 1 inch.

NEEDLES: Circular needle, 16-in length, and one set (5 needles) of dpn, both size 6, or size needed to knit to gauge.
(For equivalent Canadian/ British and metric needle sizes, see page 88.)

Lace Rib Watch Cap

Another single-color watch cap, this one is knit with a decorative Lace Rib pattern. (Pictured on page 21.)

For information on converting measurements and yarn weights to metric, see page 88.

SIZES: Small (Large, X-Large). Cap circumference 16²/₃ (20, 23¹/₃) inches.

YARN: Worsted weight, 100% wool, 4-ply, 210 to 220 yds per 3¹/₂ oz; 1 skein.

GAUGE: 6 stitches = 1 inch over Lace Rib pattern.

NEEDLES: Circular needle, 16-in length, and one set of dpn, both size 6, or size needed to knit to gauge. *(For equivalent Canadian/ British and metric needle sizes, see page 88.)*

INSTRUCTIONS

With circular needle cast on 100 (120, 140) stitches using Yarn-Over Tubular Cast-On (page 13). Join, being careful not to twist.

Cuff: Work k1, p1 rib for 4 (5, 6) inches.

Body: Work Lace Rib for 2³/₄ (3¹/₂, 4) inches, ending with last round of Lace Rib chart.

Crown: Switch to double-pointed needles now, or when there are too few stitches to support the circular needle. Work Crown chart.

Once finished, break off the yarn with an 8-inch tail and thread the end into a yarn needle. Draw the thread through remaining stitches and fasten off.

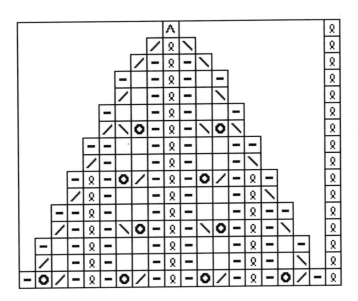

CROWN

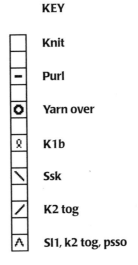

BODY

KEY

	Knit
−	Purl
O	Yarn over
Ⴥ	K1b
\	Ssk
/	K2 tog
Λ	Sl1, k2 tog, psso

Aran Watch Cap

Aran patterns create attractive garments, whether caps or sweaters. This is a simple set of patterns to work. While the cap shown is worked in traditional white, this design would be striking in a rich color as well. (Pictured on page 18.)

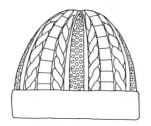

For information on converting measurements and yarn weights to metric, see page 88.

SIZES: Small (Medium, Large, X-Large). Cap circumference 16 (18, 20, 22) inches.

YARN: Worsted weight, 100% wool, 4-ply, 210 to 220 yds per 3½ oz; 1 skein.

GAUGE: 7 stitches to the inch over cable and k/p pattern.

NEEDLES: Circular needle, 16-in length, and one set of dpn, both size 6 or size needed to knit to gauge. *(For equivalent Canadian/ British and metric needle sizes, see page 88.)*

INSTRUCTIONS

With circular needle cast on 112 (124, 136, 148) stitches using Yarn-Over Tubular Cast-On (page 13). Join, being careful not to twist.

Cuff: Work k1, p1 rib for 4 (4½, 5½, 6) inches.

Body: Work pattern for your size for 4 (4½, 5, 5¾) inches.

Crown: Switch to double-pointed needles now. In order to have a neat end to the cap we will decrease rapidly over the next 4 rounds. This way, we won't have lots of plain knitting on the crown of this beautifully patterned cap. At the beginning of the round purl 2 stitches together all the way around the cap. Do this for 4 rounds.

Once finished, break off the yarn with an 8-inch tail and thread the end into a yarn needle. Draw the thread through remaining stitches and fasten off.

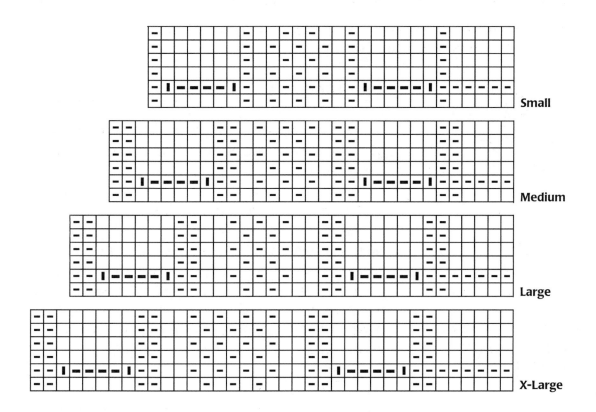

Small

Medium

Large

X-Large

KEY

☐ Knit

⊟ Purl

⊞⊟⊟⊟⊟⊞ Six-stitch cable:
Sl 3 to cable needle, hold
in front, k3, k3 from
cable needle.

All-Over Two-Color Patterned Watch Cap

The pattern works beautifully over the whole body and crown, making this a rich-looking cap. (Pictured on pages 22 and 23.)

For information on converting measurements and yarn weights to metric, see page 88.

SIZES: Small (Medium, X-Large). Cap circumference 16 (19¼, 22½) inches.

YARN: Worsted weight, 100% wool, 4-ply 210 to 220 yds per 3½ oz; 1 skein in each of 2 contrasting colors.

GAUGE: 7½ stitches and 7½ rounds = 1 inch.

NEEDLES: Circular needle, 16-in length, and one set of dpn, both size 4 or size needed to knit to gauge. *(For equivalent Canadian/British and metric needle sizes, see page 88.)*

INSTRUCTIONS

With circular needle cast on 120 (144, 168) stitches using Yarn-Over Tubular Cast-On (page 13). Join, being careful not to twist.

Cuff: Work k1, p1 rib for 4 (5, 6) inches.

Body and Crown: Work the chart beginning at the appropriate round. You will work 5 (6, 7) pattern repeats for one complete round. After the chart is complete there should be 10 (12, 14) stitches on the needles. Switch to double-pointed needles when there are too few stitches to support the circular needle.

Break off the yarn with an 8-inch tail and thread the end into a yarn needle. Draw the thread through remaining stitches and fasten off.

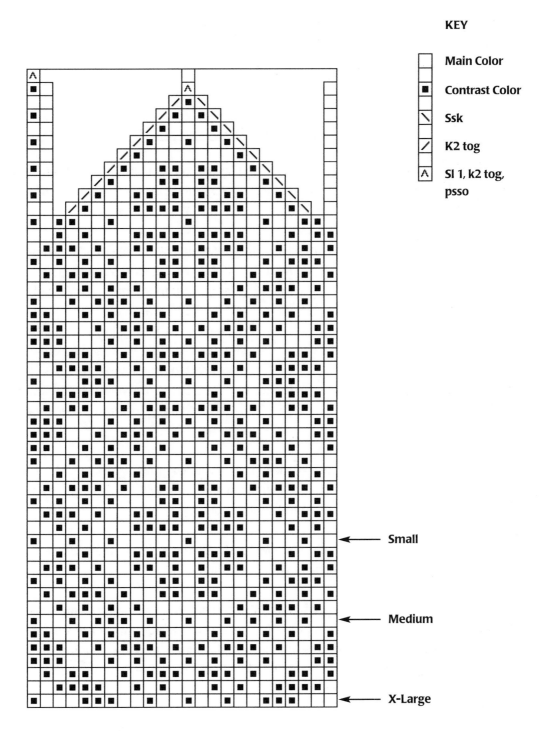

KEY

☐	Main Color
■	Contrast Color
╲	Ssk
╱	K2 tog
⋀	Sl 1, k2 tog, psso

← Small

← Medium

← X-Large

Triple-Patterned Watch Cap

The cuff in this cap is worked in stranded pattern, with the ever-popular Star motif on the crown. (Pictured on page 18.)

For information on converting measurements and yarn weights to metric, see page 88.

SIZES: Small (Medium, Large, X-Large). Cap circumference 16 (18, 20, 22) inches.

YARN: Worsted weight, 100% wool, 4-ply 210 to 220 yds per 3½ oz; 1 skein each of Main Color and Contrast Color. (White is MC and blue is CC in the example shown.)

GAUGE: 5½ stitches and 6¾ rows = 1 inch.

NEEDLES: Circular needle, 16-in length, and one set of dpn, both size 6, or size needed to knit to gauge. *(For equivalent Canadian/ British and metric needle sizes, see page 88.)*

INSTRUCTIONS

With circular needle cast on 90 (100, 110, 120) stitches in two colors using Two-Strand Cast-on (page 10). Join, being careful not to twist.

Twined Herringbone edge: Work edge of cuff as follows:
> Round 1: K1 MC, k1 CC, work around.
> Round 2: Move yarn to the front, p1 MC, set yarn just worked down to the LEFT, bring CC over, p1 CC. The working yarn will become very twisted after working this round; it will be untwisted as you work round 3.
> Round 3: P1 MC, p1 CC, set yarn just worked to the RIGHT and bring the yarn to be worked under it.

Cuff: Work 1 (1, 2, 2) rounds of MC. Work Cuff chart. Work 1 (1, 2, 2) rounds of MC. Turn. With MC knit one round, purl one round, knit 2 rounds.

Body: With MC and CC work Body chart for 3½ (4, 4¼, 4½) inches. Work one round MC.

Crown: Work Crown chart from the appropriate starting point for your size. All sizes need to work the seam stitches on the left of the chart. When working the chart for Small, Medium, or Large, do not work the first round of decreases you get to.

Once finished, break off the yarn with an 8-inch tail and thread the end into a yarn needle. Draw the thread through remaining stitches and fasten off.

Seam sts

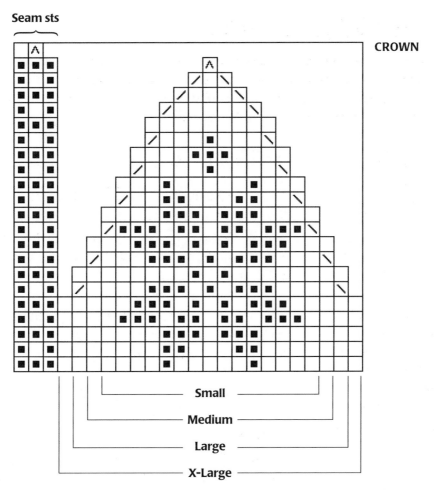

CROWN

Small

Medium

Large

X-Large

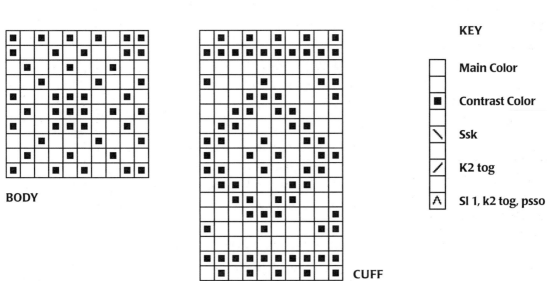

BODY

CUFF

KEY

	Main Color
■	Contrast Color
\	Ssk
/	K2 tog
ʌ	Sl 1, k2 tog, psso

Gansey Watch Cap

Gansey patterns are beautiful and create lovely caps. It is interesting to note that in all the books I've seen on Gansey sweaters, not one of the fishermen pictured is wearing a knitted cap. The Gansey sweaters were traditionally knit in a dark navy yarn. This cap is shown in white so you can see the patterning— have fun with your own color choice. (Pictured on page 20.)

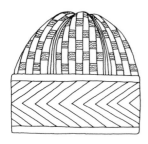

For information on converting measurements and yarn weights to metric, see page 88.

SIZES: Small (Medium, Large, X-Large) Cap circumference 16 (18, 20, 22) inches.

YARN: Worsted weight, 100% wool, 4-ply 210 to 220 yds per 3½ oz; 1 skein.

GAUGE: 6 stitches and 9 rounds = 1 inch over body pattern.

NEEDLES: Circular needle, 16-in length, and one set of dpn, both size 6, or size needed to knit to gauge. *(For equivalent Canadian/ British and metric needle sizes, see page 88.)*

INSTRUCTIONS

With circular needle cast on 96 (108, 120, 132) stitches using Two-Strand Cast-On (page 10). Join, being careful not to twist. Work 2 garter-stitch ridges plus one more knit round (knit one round, purl one round, knit one round, purl one round, knit one round).

Cuff: Work Cuff chart, choosing the appropriate size and working between the lines for that size. This will insure that the cuff pattern is centered.

Work 3 garter ridges (knit one round, purl one round is one ridge). Turn; you want to have the inside of the cuff facing out as you work the body of the cap so that the pattern will be on the outside when the cuff is turned up.

Body: Work Body chart between the lines for your size, and the 5 stitches of garter-stitch panel. Begin in the round indicated on the right side of the chart and finish at the place indicated on the left side of the chart—a total of 51 (59, 67, 74) rounds.

Crown: Switch to double-pointed needles now, or when there are too few stitches to support the circular needle.

CUFF

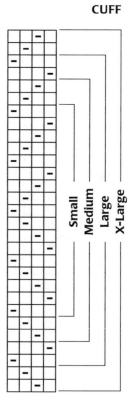

Begin working the crown chart at place indicated on the right side of the chart.

Break off the yarn with an 8-inch tail and thread the end into a yarn needle. Draw the thread through remaining stitches and fasten off.

CROWN

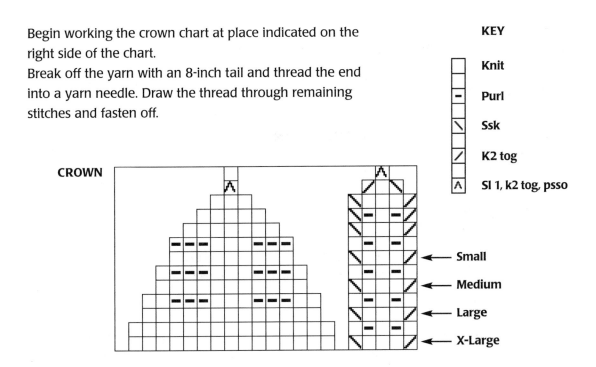

BODY Begin at round indicated on right, then work 2 (3, 4, 4) repeats of chart, and 6 (2, 2, 0) additional rounds.

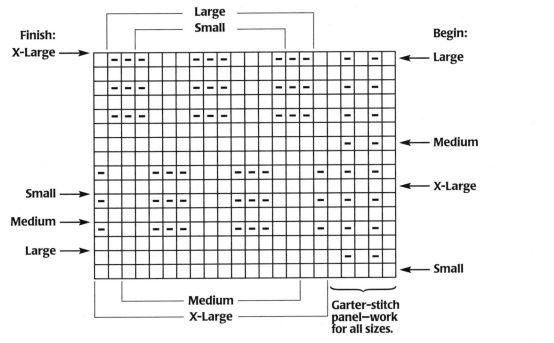

Doublemassa

This may be the warmest cap in the book, with a liner and a four-layer cuff.
(Pictured on page 20.)

For information on converting measurements and yarn weights to metric, see page 88.

SIZE: Large. Cap circumference 22 inches.

YARN: Fingering weight, approx. 230 yds per 2 oz; 2 skeins for liner and Main Color, 1 skein for Contrast Color.

GAUGE: 6½ stitches and 7½ rounds = 1 inch.

NEEDLES: Circular needle, 16-in length, and one set of dpn (5 needles), both size 4 or size needed to knit to gauge.
(For equivalent Canadian/ British and metric needle sizes, see page 88.)

INSTRUCTIONS

This cap is knit starting from the top of the head liner. Knit down to the edge of the cuff and then up to the top of the outside of the cap.

Liner: With circular needle cast on 12 stitches Using Chain Cast-On (page 9). Join, being careful not to twist.
Round 1: K2, yo, k2, yo, k4, yo, k2, yo, k2 (16 stitches).

Increase 4 stitches each round 10 times more (56 stitches). Place the increases one stitch before the end of the first and third needle and one stitch after the beginning of the second and fourth needle. You can use any increase method you like; I chose to use yarn over as it is easy to see and to count the increases.

Increase 4 stitches every other round 4 times (72 stitches), each third round 3 times (84 stitches), each fourth round 5 times (104), each fifth round one time (108 stitches).

Change the location of the increases to make them equidistant and increase 6 stitches every 6 rounds 5 times (138 stitches). Knit 8 rounds or until liner measures 10¼ inches. Increase 2 stitches in the last round (140 stitches).

Begin Pattern: Change to two colors and begin working chart. The body of the cap decreases slightly as you work up, and this happens on solid-color rounds between pattern rounds. Decrease evenly at the rounds indicated on the chart:

      A—Decrease 2 (138 stitches remain).
      B—Decrease 2 (136 stitches remain).

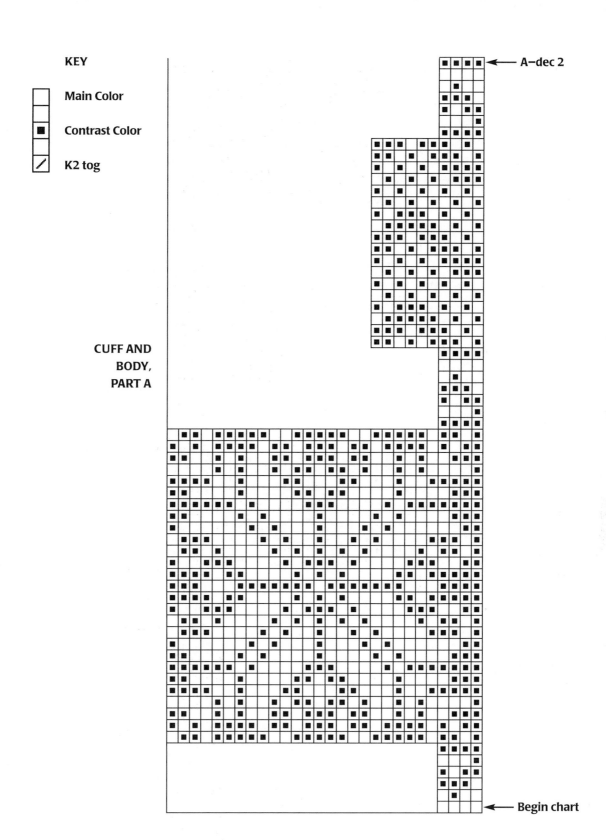

KEY

Main Color

■ Contrast Color

╱ K2 tog

CUFF AND
BODY,
PART A

← A—dec 2

← Begin chart

39

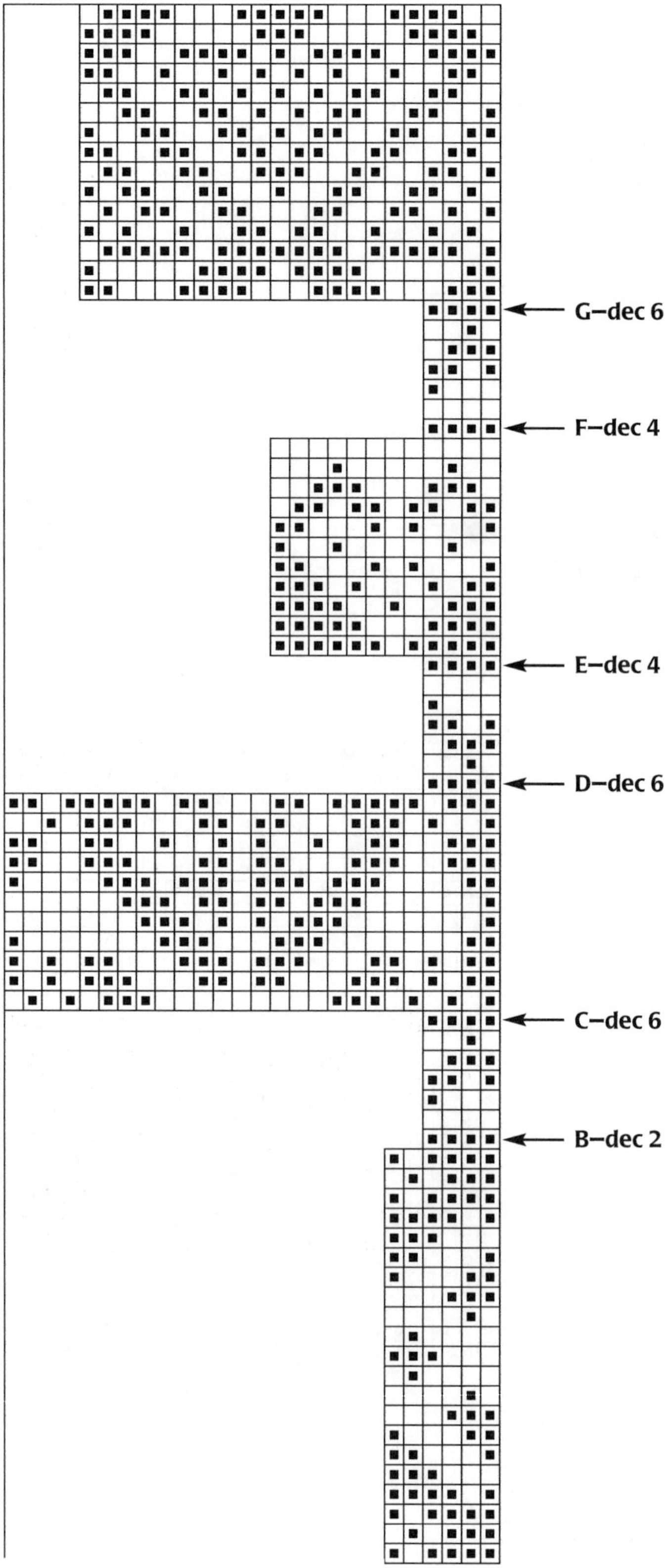

**CUFF AND
BODY,
PART B**

← G—dec 6

← F—dec 4

← E—dec 4

← D—dec 6

← C—dec 6

← B—dec 2

C—Decrease 6 (130 stitches remain).
D—Decrease 6 (124 stitches remain).
E—Decrease 4 (120 stitches remain).
F—Decrease 4 (116 stitches remain).
G—Decrease 6 (110 stitches remain).

Once you have finished the Body chart, knit one round using MC and decrease 2 stitches evenly in this round (108 sts).

Crown: Switch to double-pointed needles now, or when there are too few stitches to support the circular needle. Work the crown chart. Break off the yarn with an 8-inch tail and thread the end into a yarn needle. Draw the thread through remaining stitches and fasten off.

Tassel: Follow tassel directions on page 14, but make the tassel slightly larger by wrapping the yarn 60 times around a 6-inch piece of cardboard rather than 40 times around a 4-inch cardboard.

CROWN

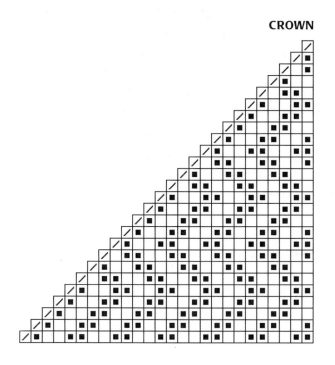

KEY

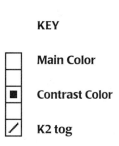

Main Color

Contrast Color

K2 tog

Norwegian Star

Creating a hem instead of folded cuff leaves more room on the cap for pattern knitting.
(Pictured on page 19.)

For information on converting measurements and yarn weights to metric, see page 88.

SIZES: Small, Med., Large. Cap circumference 16 (18²/₃, 21¹/₃) inches.

YARN: Worsted weight, 100% wool, 4-ply 210 to 220 yds per 3¹/₂ oz; 1 skein each of Main Color and Contrast Color.

GAUGE: 6 stitches and 7¹/₄ rounds = 1 inch over Star pattern using larger needle.

NEEDLES: Circular needle, 16-in length, sizes 4 and 6, or size needed to knit to gauge, and one set of dpn in larger size.
(For equivalent Canadian/ British and metric needle sizes, see page 88.)

INSTRUCTIONS

With smaller circular needle and MC cast on 96 (112, 128) stitches using Chain Cast-On (page 9). Join, being careful not to twist.

Hem: Work 2³/₄, (3, 3¹/₂) inches stockinette stitch.

Turning round: *Yo, k2 tog*, repeat around.

Body: Change to larger needle and work from the Body chart for 2³/₄ (3, 3¹/₂) inches.

NOTE: You have two options for securing the hem to the cap. You may either wait until the cap is complete and then sew the hem in place or you may knit the hem to the cap when you reach the point where the hem and the body are the same length. Instructions follow for the latter technique, which joins the hem in an absolutely straight line, invisible from the outside of the cap, and minimizes finishing.

Securing the hem as you knit: With a double-pointed needle, pick up one stitch along the cast-on edge for every stitch cast on; knit each stitch with its corresponding live stitch (and maintain the pattern of the body of the cap). It may be easier to pick up one stitch at a time rather than picking up a needleful.

Size Large Only: Work one repeat of the Lice pattern after finishing the Body chart.

Crown: Switch to double-pointed needles now, or when there are too few stitches to support the circular needle. Work one round in MC and decrease 5 (0, 2) stitches evenly

spaced over the round 91 (112, 126) stitches. Begin working
the Crown chart at the proper place for your size.
Once finished, break off the yarn with an 8-inch tail and
thread the end into a yarn needle. Draw the thread through
remaining stitches and fasten off.

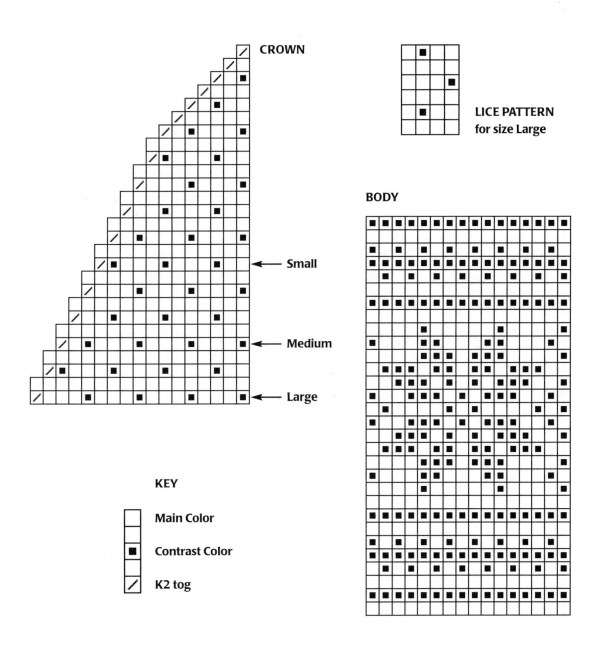

CROWN

LICE PATTERN
for size Large

BODY

← Small

← Medium

← Large

KEY

☐ Main Color

■ Contrast Color

╱ K2 tog

Komi Cap

The Komi, who live in Northeast European Russia, developed a system of color knitting that was simple to remember and created beautiful and complicated patterns. This one is shown on p. 44 of Mostly Mittens: Traditional Knitting Patterns from Russia's Komi People, *Lark Books, 1998. (Pictured on page 21.)*

For information on converting measurements and yarn weights to metric, see page 88.

SIZES: Child (Adult). Cap circumference 18 (21) inches.

YARN: Fingering weight, 310 yds per 50 g (1¾ oz); 1 skein in each of 2 contrasting colors. (Ash and Olive shown.)

GAUGE: 10 stitches and 10 rounds = 1 inch.

NEEDLES: Circular needle, 16-in length, sizes 0 and 1, or size needed to knit to gauge; and one set of dpn in larger size.
(For equivalent Canadian/ British and metric needle sizes, see page 88.)

INSTRUCTIONS

With circular needle and MC cast on 160 (190) stitches using Chain Cast-On (page 9). Join, being careful not to twist.

Hem: Knit in MC stockinette stitch for 2 (2½) inches. In the next round knit around and increase 20 (30) stitches evenly around. Purl one round.

Body and Crown: Change to larger needle and begin working the chart at the bottom right of the chart for Adult size, or 17 rounds up for Child's size. For Child's size the pattern is repeated 6 times per round, and for Adult's size it is repeated 7 times. The chart has one extra column to the left; this is the LAST stitch of the ROUND (not of the pattern repeat, but of the round). This stitch is different to help eliminate the jog that happens when knitting patterns in the round.

When you have knit 2 (2½) inches of the chart, work the hem in the next round by using a double-pointed needle to pick up stitches along the cast-on edge and knit them together with their corresponding live stitches in the body of the cap (maintaining the color pattern). This method joins the hem invisibly in a straight line and minimizes finishing. Because the body of the cap at this point has more stitches than the cast-on edge, you will occasionally have to knit a single, unpaired stitch.

Child size: *k8 of hem and body tog, k1 of body alone*; repeat around.

Adult size: *k6 of hem and body tog, k1 of body alone*; end with k10 of hem and body tog.

Continue following the chart, switching to double-pointed needles now, or when there are too few stitches to support the circular needle.

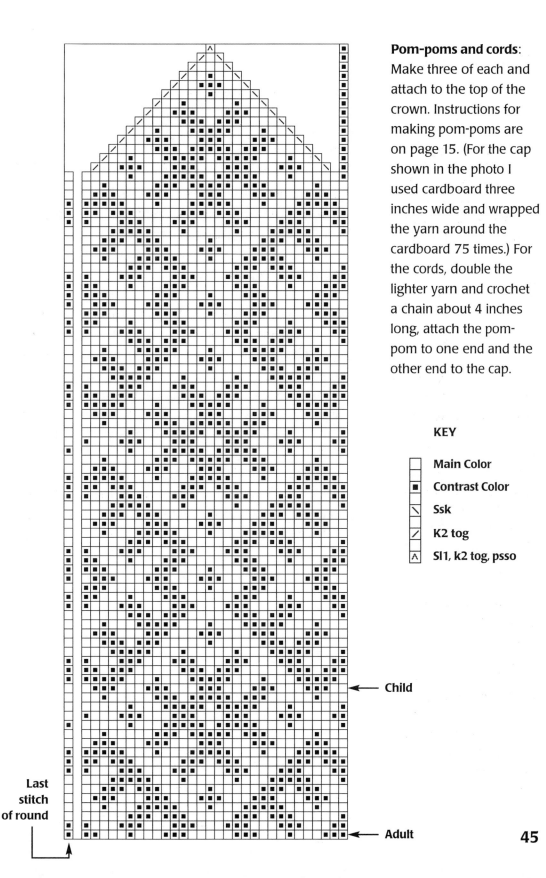

Pom-poms and cords: Make three of each and attach to the top of the crown. Instructions for making pom-poms are on page 15. (For the cap shown in the photo I used cardboard three inches wide and wrapped the yarn around the cardboard 75 times.) For the cords, double the lighter yarn and crochet a chain about 4 inches long, attach the pom-pom to one end and the other end to the cap.

KEY

☐	Main Color
■	Contrast Color
⟍	Ssk
⟋	K2 tog
⋀	Sl1, k2 tog, psso

Child

Last stitch of round

Adult

45

Fana Cap

The Scandinavian patterns are relatively simple, and are perennial favorites. (Pictured on page 17.)

For information on converting measurements and yarn weights to metric, see page 88.

SIZES: Small (Medium, Large, X-Large). Cap circumference 16 (18, 20, 22) inches.

YARN: Worsted weight, 100% wool, 210 yds per 3½ oz; 1 skein each of 2 contrasting colors. (Gray and Green shown in photo.)

GAUGE: 6 stitches and 7¼ rounds = 1 inch over Star pattern.

NEEDLES: Circular needle, 16-in length, and one set of dpn, both size 6, or size needed to knit to gauge. *(For equivalent Canadian/ British and metric needle sizes, see page 88.)*

INSTRUCTIONS

With circular needle and MC cast on 96 (108, 120, 132) stitches using Two-Strand Cast-On for knit and purl ribbing (page 11). Join, being careful not to twist.

Cuff: Work k1b, p1 rib for 1 inch.

Body: Work Body chart for the rows indicated for your size. For Medium and X-Large, decrease 4 stitches evenly spaced in the last round of body before beginning the Crown chart.

Crown: Work the Crown chart beginning at the appropriate place for your size. Switch to double-pointed needles now, or when there are too few stitches to support the circular needle.

Break off the yarn with an 8-inch tail and thread the end into a yarn needle. Draw the thread through remaining stitches and fasten off.

CROWN

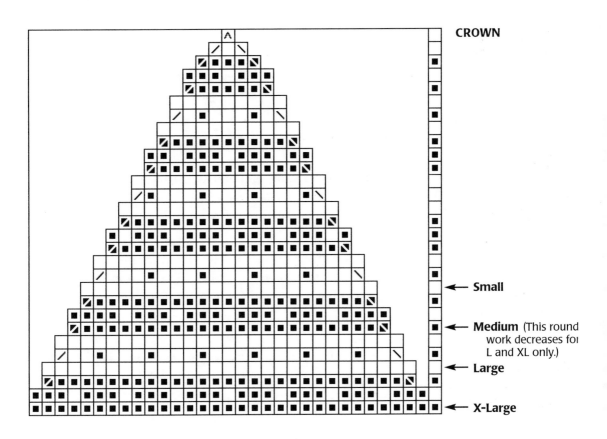

← Small

← Medium (This round work decreases for L and XL only.)

← Large

← X-Large

BODY

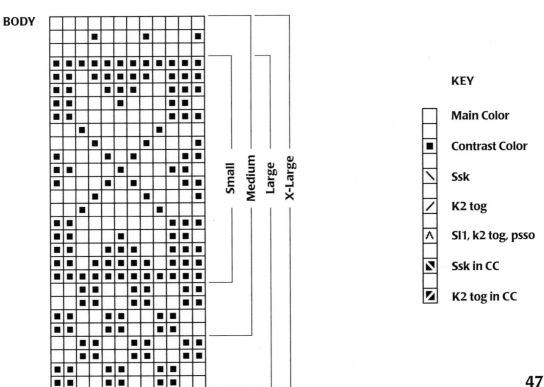

Small

Medium

Large

X-Large

KEY

☐	Main Color
■	Contrast Color
╲	Ssk
╱	K2 tog
⋀	Sl1, k2 tog, psso
◨	Ssk in CC
◪	K2 tog in CC

47

Ullared Cap

These patterns are taken from one of the most beautiful of the nineteenth century's Swedish sweaters. The red and black combination is a perennial favorite. (Pictured on pages 22 and 23.)

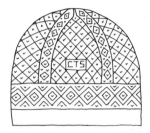

For information on converting measurements and yarn weights to metric, see page 88.

SIZES: Small (Medium, Large, X-Large). Cap circumference 16 (18, 20, 22) inches.

YARN: Sport weight, 100% wool, 5-ply, 246 yds per 3½ oz; 1 skein each of Main Color (red), and Contrast Color (black).

GAUGE: 8 stitches and 10 rounds = 1 inch over cuff pattern.

NEEDLES: Circular needle, 16-in length, and one set of dpn, both size 4, or size needed to knit to gauge. *(For equivalent Canadian/ British and metric needle sizes, see page 88.)*

INSTRUCTIONS

With circular needle and CC cast on 130 (140, 160, 180) stitches using Two-Strand Cast-On, k1, p1 (page 11). Join, being careful not to twist.

Cuff: Work k1b, p1 rib for 1 inch. Join the MC and begin knitting from the lower right-hand corner from the Cuff chart. Continue repeating the chart all the way around the cap until the last round of the cuff chart.

As you work the last round of the chart, you need to either increase or decrease the following number of stitches: −2 (+4, 0, −4). Total stitches 128 (144, 160, 176).

Body and Crown: Work the Crown chart between the lines for your size. Begin knitting at the lower right hand corner, repeating the pattern four times each round. The crown consists of 4 broad panels of a light-on-dark diamond pattern separated by narrow vertical bands of dark-on-light diamonds. Begin working the chart with a narrow band. A charming option is to work the hat owner's initials into one of the 4 broad panels (see page 50).

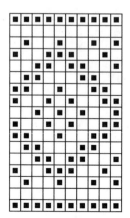

CUFF

KEY

☐	Main Color
▪	Contrast Color
⧅	Ssk
⧄	K2 tog
⋀	Sl1, k2 tog in MC
◪	Ssk in CC
◪	K2 tog in CC
◪	Sl1, K2 tog, psso in CC

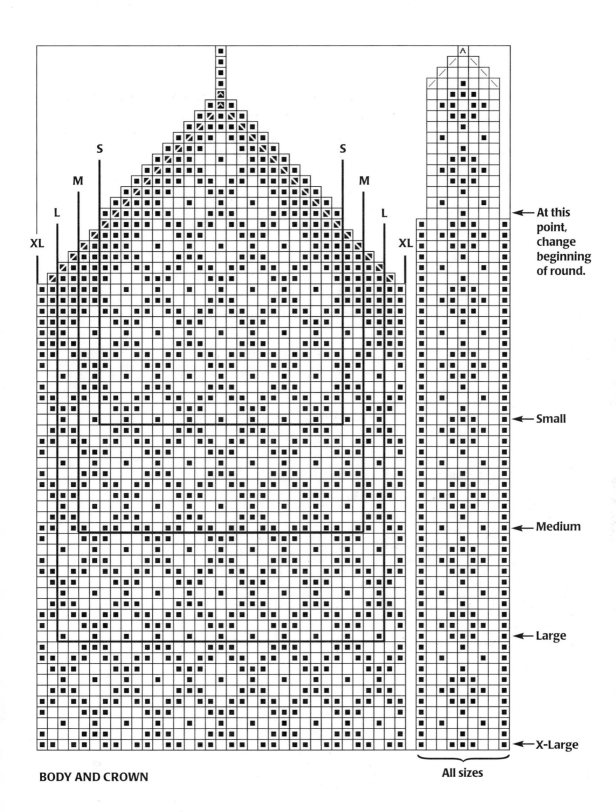

BODY AND CROWN

At this point, change beginning of round.

Small

Medium

Large

X-Large

All sizes

49

Including initials on crown: Refer to the Alphabet chart if you wish to include initials. Each letter is 3 stitches wide by 5 rows high and will fit into one of the shaded areas of the Initials Box chart. Insert this initials box in the center of the first panel, starting in the fifth round of the Crown chart (work the other three panels with just the diamond pattern— no initials).

NOTE: It will be easier to make the change to double-pointed needles when you begin the decrease rounds of the crown rather than waiting until you have too few stitches to work comfortably with the circular needle.

Finishing: When you have 8 stitches left, break off both yarns with tails of about 8 inches and thread the ends one at a time into a yarn needle. Draw the thread through remaining stitches and fasten off.

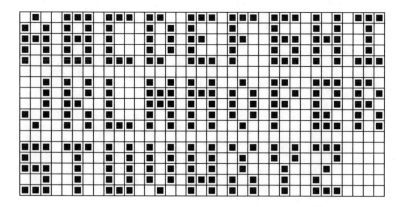

ALPHABET

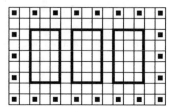

INITIALS BOX

Lusekofte Cap

Norwegian motifs are what we most often think of when ski sweaters and caps are mentioned. I've included two of the popular patterns for this cap: the zig-zag often seen at the top of sleeves, and the X-pattern used across the shoulders of a Lusekofte sweater. (Pictured on pages 21 and 22.)

INSTRUCTIONS

With circular needle and MC (darker color) cast on 96 (108, 120, 132) stitches using Two-Strand Cast-On, k1, p1 (page 11). Join, being careful not to twist.

Cuff: Using MC work k1b, p1 rib for 1 inch.

Body: Work Body chart. If you prefer, you may substitute one of the X-patterns for the zig-zag portion of the Body chart.

Crown: Switch to double-pointed needles now, or when there are too few stitches to support the circular needle. After you have finished the body, begin working the crown at the appropriate spot for the size you are working.

Break off the yarn with an 8-inch tail and thread the end into a yarn needle. Draw the thread through remaining stitches and fasten off.

Tassel and cord: Instructions for making tassels appear on page 12. Attach tassel with either a Lanyard Braid (page 15) or a Twisted Cord (page 15).

For information on converting measurements and yarn weights to metric, see page 88.

SIZES: Small (Medium, Large, X-Large). Cap circumference 16 (18, 20, 22) inches.

YARN: Worsted weight, 100% wool, 4-ply, 210 to 220 yds per 3½ oz; 1 skein each of 2 contrasting colors.

GAUGE: 6 stitches and 7¼ rounds = 1 inch.

NEEDLES: Circular needle, 16-in length, and one set (5 needles) of dpn, both size 6, or size needed to knit to gauge.
(For equivalent Canadian/ British and metric needle sizes, see page 88.)

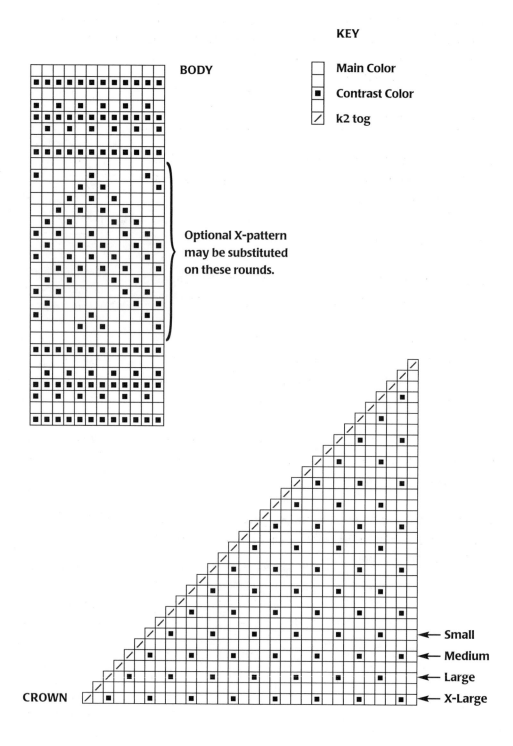

KEY

Main Color

Contrast Color

k2 tog

BODY

Optional X-pattern
may be substituted
on these rounds.

Small

Medium

Large

X-Large

CROWN

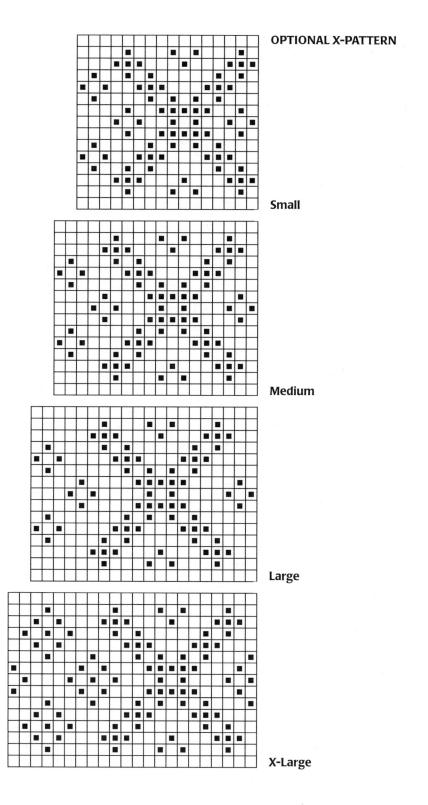

OPTIONAL X-PATTERN

Small

Medium

Large

X-Large

53

Fair Isle Cap

The magic of the Fair Isle patterns is that, though they look complex, only two colors are used in any given row. (Pictured on page 20.)

For information on converting measurements and yarn weights to metric, see page 88.

SIZES: Small (Medium, Large, X-Large). Cap circumference 16 (18, 20, 22) inches.

YARN: Sport weight, 185 yds per 50 g (1¾ oz), 1 skein each of Lt. Gray (Main Color), Dk. Gray, Lt. Rose, Dk. Rose, Turquoise.

GAUGE: 8 stitches and 8 rounds = 1 inch.

NEEDLES: Circular needle, 16-in length, and one set of dpn, both size 4, or size needed to knit to gauge. *(For equivalent Canadian/ British and metric needle sizes, see page 88.)*

INSTRUCTIONS

With circular needle and Lt. Gray (MC) cast on 128 (144, 160, 176) stitches using Two-Strand Cast-On for knit and purl ribbing (page 10). Join, being careful not to twist.

Cuff: Work corrugated ribbing—k 2, p2, always using MC for the knit stitches and CC for the purl stitches. Work 2 rounds with Turquoise for the contrast color, then 1 round with Dk. Rose, 3 rounds with Lt. Rose, 1 round with Dark Rose, 2 rounds with Turquoise.

Body: Begin working body chart. Work between lines as appropriate.

Crown: Switch to double-pointed needles now, or when there are too few stitches to support the circular needle. Work the appropriate crown chart for your size (8 repeats on each crown).

Break off the yarn with an 8-inch tail and thread the end into a yarn needle. Draw the thread through remaining stitches and fasten off.

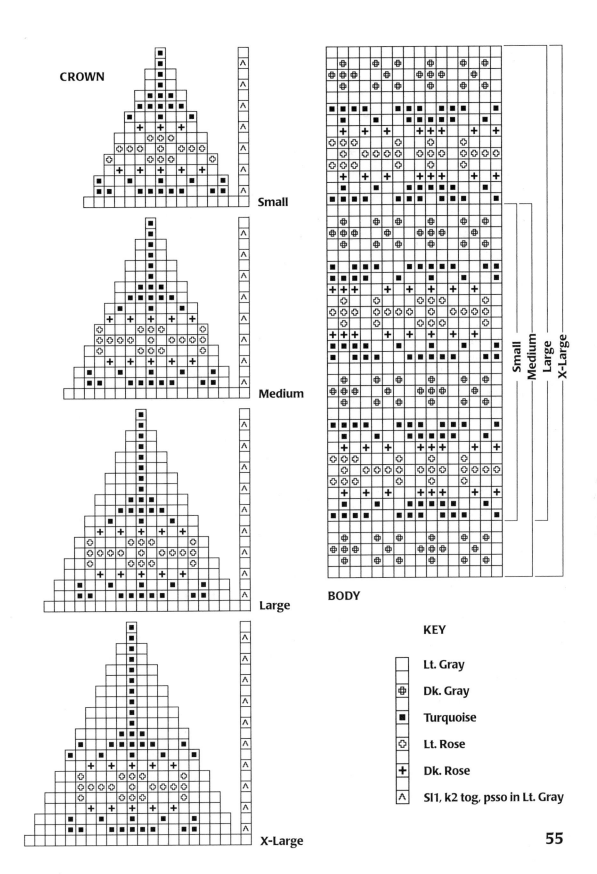

CROWN

Small

Medium

Large

X-Large

BODY

Small
Medium
Large
X-Large

KEY

	Lt. Gray
⊕	Dk. Gray
■	Turquoise
✿	Lt. Rose
+	Dk. Rose
∧	Sl1, k2 tog, psso in Lt. Gray

Tassled Fez

The Turkish motifs I found in a book of sock patterns intrigued me. It is fun to adapt these patterns for caps as well as sweaters. (Pictured on page 19.)

For information on converting measurements and yarn weights to metric, see page 88.

SIZES: Small (Medium, Large, X-Large). Cap circumference 16 (18, 20, 22) inches.

YARN: Worsted weight, 100% wool, 4-ply, 210 to 220 yds per 3½ oz; 1 skein each of 2 contrasting colors.

GAUGE 6 stitches = 1 inch over 2-color pattern.

NEEDLES: Circular needle, 16-in length, and one set of dpn, both size 4, or size needed to knit to gauge. *(For equivalent Canadian/British and metric needle sizes, see page 88.)*

INSTRUCTIONS

With circular needle cast on 96 (108, 120, 132) stitches Using Two-Strand Cast-On, Two-Color (page 11). Join, being careful not to twist.

Cuff: Work Twined Herringbone edge:
> Round 1: K1 MC, k1 CC, work around.
> Round 2: Move yarn to the front, p1 MC, set yarn just worked down to the LEFT bring CC over, p1 CC. The working yarn will become very twisted after working this round; they will be untwisted in working round 3.
> Round 3: P1 MC, p1 CC, set yarn just worked to the RIGHT and bring the yarn to be worked under it.

Body: Begin working appropriate chart for your size and continue until piece measures 6 (7, 8, 9) inches. The pattern repeats three times around the body of the cap. Bind off loosely.

Sewing the Crown: The finished Fez has a three-pointed top—each point aligns at the center of a pattern repeat. Turn cap inside out. With a tapestry needle and piece of yarn about 24 inches long, count back 16 (18, 20, 22) sts from the end of the cast off. Begin by sewing that stitch and the following stitch together to form the tip of one point, then work back to where you began counting, sewing the edge stitches together. (You now have completed one point of the three). Take the middle stitch of what is unsewn and bring it in to the center of the crown, forming two more points. Sew the second point from the center out to the end. Break off the

yarn, reattach it at the center of the crown, and sew the third point from the center out to the end.
Weave in all the ends.

Tassels: Make three tassels according to the instructions on page 14 and attach to the points of the fez using the cord of your choice. Finger Crochet cord (page 15) was used for the example shown in the photograph.

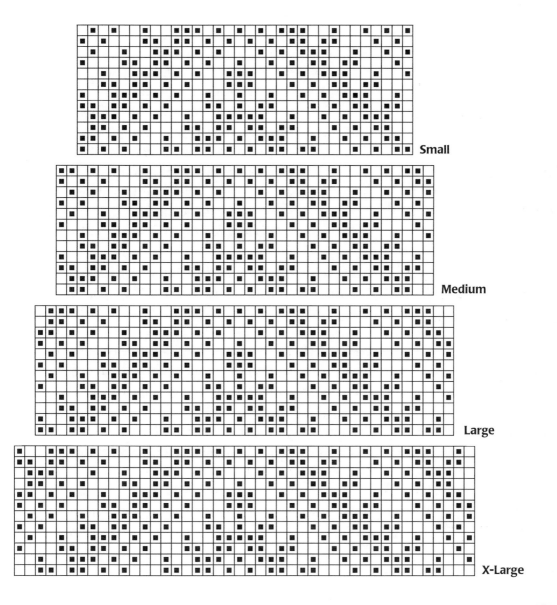

Small

Medium

Large

X-Large

Turkish-Patterned Cap

This is another Turkish pattern originally from a sock. The cap is worked with a shaped crown that features an attractive star design. (Pictured on page 17.)

For information on converting measurements and yarn weights to metric, see page 88.

SIZES: Small (Medium, Large, X-Large). Cap circumference 16 (18, 20, 22) inches.

YARN: Worsted weight, 210 yds per 3½ oz; one skein of Main Color and one of Contrast Color (White and Navy in the example shown).

GAUGE: Over pattern, 7 stitches and 8 rows = 1 inch.

NEEDLES: Circular needle, 16-in length, and one set of dpn, both size 4, or size needed to knit to gauge. *(For equivalent Canadian/ British and metric needle sizes, see page 88.)*

INSTRUCTIONS

With circular needle cast on 112, (126, 140, 154) stitches Using Two-Strand Cast-On, Two-Color (page 11). Join, being careful not to twist.

Cuff: Work Twined Herringbone edge:

Round 1: K1 MC, k1 CC, work around.

Round 2: Move yarn to the front, p1 MC, set yarn just worked down to the LEFT bring CC over, p1 CC. The working yarn will become very twisted after working this round; it will be untwisted as you work round 3.

Round 3: P1 MC, p1 CC, set yarn just worked to the RIGHT and bring the yarn to be worked under it.

Body: K 1 round of CC. Begin at the spot indicated for the size you are working and work to top of pattern. And then work 1 (1, 2, 2) repeats of the 22-round Body pattern.

Crown: Switch to double-pointed needles now, or when there are too few stitches to support the circular needle. Work the crown decreases portion of the chart.

Break off the yarn with an 8-inch tail and thread the end into a yarn needle. Draw the thread through remaining stitches and fasten off.

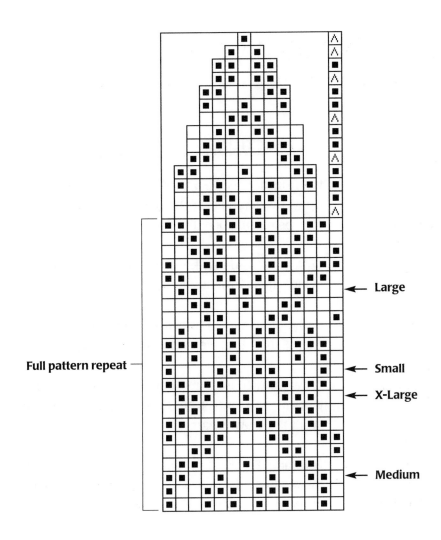

Full pattern repeat

← Large

← Small

← X-Large

← Medium

KEY

	Main color
	Contrast Color
	Sl1, k2 tog, psso in CC

Cap with Slip-Stitch Cable

Using slip stitches creates a more prominent cable against the reverse stockinette ground.
(Pictured on page 18.)

For information on converting measurements and yarn weights to metric, see page 88.

SIZES: Small (Medium, Large). Cap circumference 16 (19, 22) inches.

YARN: 100% wool, 4-ply, approx. 175 yds per 3½ oz; 1 skein each of 3 colors: Gray (MC), Blue, and White.

GAUGE: 5½ stitches = 1 inch over Slip-Stitch Cable pattern. Row gauge 16 rows = 1½ inches.

NEEDLES: Circular needle, 16-in length, and one set of dpn, both size 8, or size needed to knit to gauge. *(For equivalent Canadian/ British and metric needle sizes, see page 88.)*

INSTRUCTIONS

With circular needle and MC cast on 88 (104, 120) stitches Using Two-Strand Cast-On for knit and purl ribbing (page 11). Join, being careful not to twist.

Cuff: Work 4 rounds k1, p1 rib in Gray, then work 2 rounds in blue, then 2 rounds in Gray.

Body: Work 3 (4, 5) complete repeats of the Slip-Stitch Cable chart 5 (6½, 8) inches from the beginning.

Crown: Switch to double-pointed needles now, or when there are too few stitches to support the circular needle. Work the Crown chart.

Finishing: Break off the yarn with an 8-inch tail and thread the end into a yarn needle. Draw the thread through remaining stitches and fasten off.

SLIP-STITCH CABLE

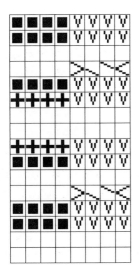

CROWN

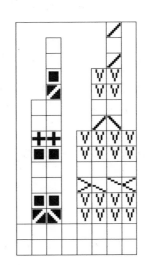

KEY

White−knit	
Sl1	
K2 tog−White	
Ssk−White	
Blue−purl	
Gray−purl	
P2 tog−Gray	
P2 tog tbl−Gray	
Cable with 4 sts; sl2 st to cable needle and hold in front, k2, k2 from cable needle.	

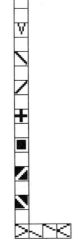

Bohus-Patterned Cap

The Bohus patterns create interest by using multiple colors and adding purl stitches to create texture at the color change line. The evenly spaced decrease lines make a subtle but pleasing sunburst pattern on the crown of this cap. (Pictured on page 19.)

For information on converting measurements and yarn weights to metric, see page 88.

SIZES: Small (Medium, Large, X-Large). Cap circumference 16 (18, 20, 22) inches.

YARN: Shetland jumper weight yarn, 150 yds per 1 oz; 1 skein each of 7 colors.*

GAUGE: 8½ stitches = 1 inch.

NEEDLES: Circular needle, 16-in length, and one set of dpn, both size 2, or size needed to knit to gauge. *(For equivalent Canadian/ British and metric needle sizes, see page 88.)*

INSTRUCTIONS

With circular needle and MC cast on 136 (152, 168, 184) stitches Using Two-Strand Cast-On (page 10). Join, being careful not to twist

Cuff: With MC, work 1 inch of garter stitch: knit one round, purl one round.

Body: Follow chart. For Large and X-Large, work the full chart; for the two smaller sizes, begin working at the place indicated.

Crown: Decrease 4 (8, 0, 4) stitches on the next round, to produce a number of stitches divisible by twelve—32 (144, 168, 180). Switch to double-pointed needles now, or when there are too few stitches to support the circular needle.

> Round 1: *K9 (10, 12, 13), k2 tog*; repeat around.
> Round 2 and all even-numbered rounds: Knit even.
> Round 3: *K8 (9, 11, 12), k2 tog*; repeat around.
> All remaining odd-numbered rounds: Continue decreasing 1 stitch at each of the 12 established decrease points until 12 stitches remain.

Change to double-pointed needles when there are not enough stitches to fit around the circular needle.

Once finished, break off the yarn with an 8-inch tail and thread the end into a yarn needle. Draw the thread through remaining stitches and fasten off.

*Example shown was made from Jamieson & Smith jumper weight wool, using Pale Peach 53 (Main Color), Flame FC7, Bright Pink 95, Butter 66, Mink 61, Mandarin 90, and Lilac FC21.

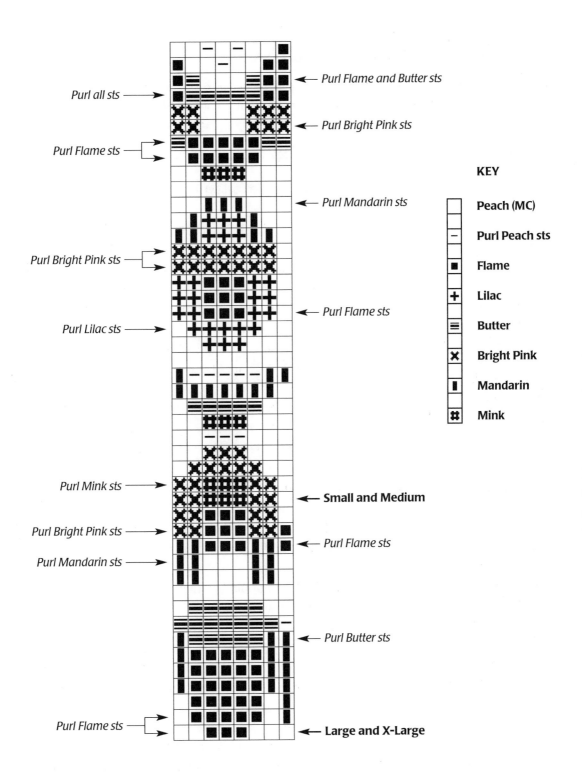

Purl all sts →

← Purl Flame and Butter sts

← Purl Bright Pink sts

Purl Flame sts →

← Purl Mandarin sts

Purl Bright Pink sts →

← Purl Flame sts

Purl Lilac sts →

Purl Mink sts →

← **Small and Medium**

Purl Bright Pink sts →

← Purl Flame sts

Purl Mandarin sts →

← Purl Butter sts

Purl Flame sts →

← **Large and X-Large**

KEY

☐	**Peach (MC)**
−	**Purl Peach sts**
■	**Flame**
+	**Lilac**
≡	**Butter**
✖	**Bright Pink**
▮	**Mandarin**
✳	**Mink**

Cap with Turk's Head Cuff

The cuff of this cap is a horizontally worked Braided Cable that looks like the macraméd Turk's Head. Rapid decreases at the top create a softly pleated crown. (Pictured on page 19.)

For information on converting measurements and yarn weights to metric, see page 88.

SIZES: Small (Medium, Large, X-Large). Cap circumference 16 (18, 20, 22) inches.

YARN: Worsted weight, 100% wool, 4-ply, 210 to 220 yds per 3½ oz; 1 skein.

GAUGE: 6 stitches = 1 inch.

NEEDLES: Circular needle, 16-in, and one set of dpn, both size 4, or size needed to knit to gauge.
(For equivalent Canadian/ British and metric needle sizes, see page 88.)

INSTRUCTIONS

With circular needle cast on 17 stitches. (Chain Cast-On, p. 9.)

Cuff: Work 16 (18, 20, 22) repeats of the Turk's Head Braid cable, beginning with a wrong-side row. (*C6F*: Slip 3 stitches to dpn and hold in front, knit 3 stitches from the left needle, knit 3 stitches from the dpn. *C6B*: Slip 3 stitches to dpn and hold in back, knit 3 stitches from the left needle, knit 3 stitches from the dpn.)

> Row 1 and all wrong-side rows: P1, k3, p9, k3, p1.
> Row 2: K1, p3, C6F, k3, p3, k1.
> Row 4: K1, p3, k9, p3, k1.
> Row 6: K1, p3, k3, C6B, p3, k1.
> Row 8: K1, p3, k9, p3, k1.

Bind off the 17 stitches and sew the ends together.

Body: Pick up and knit 96 (108, 120, 132) stitches on the right side of the braid. (Pick up 3 of every 4 stitches.) Knit in stockinette stitch until piece measures 5¾ (6½, 7½, 8½) inches including the Turk's Head cuff.

Crown: Switch to double-pointed needles and begin decreasing to shape crown. When a round has an odd number of stitches, just knit the last stitch by itself.

> Row 1: K2 tog across round. 48 (54, 60, 66 stitches).
> Row 2: K2 tog across round. 24 (27, 30, 33 stitches).
> Row 3: K2 tog across round. 12 (13, 15, 16 stitches), ending with k0 (1, 0, 1).
> Row 4: K2 tog across round. 6 (7, 7, 8 stitches), ending with k0 (0, 1, 1).

Once finished, break off the yarn with an 8-inch tail and thread the end into a yarn needle. Draw the thread through remaining stitches and fasten off.

Tam

A tam is really a FAT cap. It is a good design for women who don't want their hair crushed under a tighter cap. The I-cord on top gives it something of a Parisian look. (Pictured on page 19.)

INSTRUCTIONS

With smaller circular needle cast on 76 (88, 96, 104) stitches using Two-Strand Cast-On for knit and purl ribbing (page 11). Join, being careful not to twist.

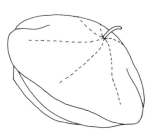

Cuff: Work in k1b, p1 rib for 1 inch.

Body: Change to larger circular needle and begin working in stockinette stitch.

> Round 1: *K1, inc 1 by knitting into front and back of next stitch,* repeat around, for a total of 114 (132, 144, 156) stitches.
>
> Round 2: Work even.

Continue to work even until total length measures 2¾, (3, 3½, 4) inches.

Crown: (Change to double-pointed needles when the decreasing number of stitches makes it necessary.)

> Round 1: [k17 (20, 22, 24), k2 tog] 6 times—108 (126, 138, 150) stitches.
>
> Round 2: Work even.
>
> Round 3: [k16 (19, 21, 23), k2 tog] 6 times—102 (120, 132, 144) stitches.
>
> Round 4: Work even.
>
> Subsequent odd rounds: Continue to decrease 6 stitches as described above, having one less stitch between decreases on each decrease round.
>
> Subsequent even rounds: Work even.

Continued on next page.

For information on converting measurements and yarn weights to metric, see page 88.

SIZES: Small (Medium, Large, X-Large). Cap circumference at cuff 16 (18, 20, 22) inches.

YARN: Worsted weight 100% wool, 4-ply, 210 to 220 yds per 3½ oz; 1 skein.

GAUGE: 5½ stitches and 8 rounds = 1 inch.

NEEDLES: Circular needle, 16-in length, sizes 4 and 6, or sizes needed to knit to gauge; and one set of dpn in larger size.
(For equivalent Canadian/ British and metric needle sizes, see page 88.)

When 66 stitches remain and last work-even round is complete, decrease 6 stitches every round until 6 stitches remain. Knit 2 together around—3 stitches.

With two double-pointed needles work about an inch of I-cord: Knit the 3 stitches on the left needle to the right, do not turn the work, but slide the 3 stitches to the other end of the needle and repeat. Be sure to pull the yarn tight on the first stitch. You are creating a small tube of circular knitting. Finish cord by knitting 3 together. Fasten off.

Rolled-Cuff Cap with Star Crown

This one is fun because it is different from many caps; the star design is on the crown instead of the cuff or body. Starting the work without ribbing makes the fabric roll, creating a cloche-type cap. (Pictured on page 21.)

INSTRUCTIONS

With circular needle and MC cast on 95 (105, 115, 125) stitches using Chain Cast-On (page 9). Join, being careful not to twist.

Body: Work stockinette stitch for 7 (7¾, 8½, 9¼) inches.

Crown: Switch to double-pointed needles now, or when there are too few stitches to support the circular needle. Work the Crown chart with MC and CC, beginning at the appropriate spot for the size you are working.

Once finished, break off the yarn with a tail about 8 inches long and thread the end into a yarn needle. Draw the thread through remaining stitches and fasten off.

KEY

☐	MC
■	CC
⟍	Ssk
⟋	K2 tog
⋀	Sl1, k2 tog, psso
◨	Ssk in CC
◪	K2 tog in cc

For information on converting measurements and yarn weights to metric, see page 88.

SIZES: Small (Medium, Large, X-Large). Cap circumference 16 (18, 20, 22) inches.

YARN: Worsted weight 100% wool, 4-ply, 210 to 220 yds per 3½ oz; 1 skein of Main Color (dark) and a few yards of the Contrast Color.

GAUGE: 5½ stitches = 1 inch.

NEEDLES: Circular needle, 16-in length, and one set of dpn, both size 6, or size needed to knit to gauge. *(For equivalent Canadian/ British and metric needle sizes, see page 88.)*

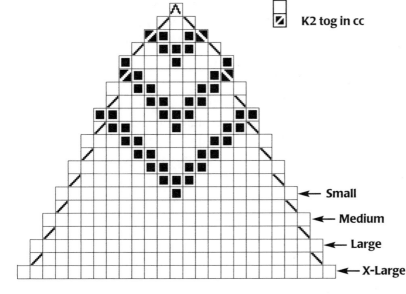

← Small

← Medium

← Large

← X-Large

Andean Cap with Earflaps

Earflaps and traditional patterns from the Andes make this a distinctive-looking cap. I based the earflaps on ones shown in Andean Folk Knitting Traditions, *by Cynthia Le Count (St. Paul, Minn.: Dos Tejedoras, 1993). (Pictured on page 21.)*

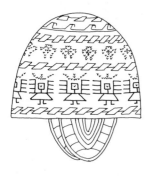

For information on converting measurements and yarn weights to metric, see page 88.

SIZE: Large. Cap circumference 20 inches.

YARN: Worsted weight 100% wool, 4-ply, 210 to 220 yds per 3½ oz; 1 skein of Black and 1 oz each of White, Gray, Burgundy, and Pink.

GAUGE: 6 stitches = 1 inch over pattern.

NEEDLES: Circular needle, 16-in length, and one set of dpn, both size 6, or size needed to knit to gauge, crochet hook size D.
(For equivalent Canadian/ British and metric needle sizes, see page 88.)

INSTRUCTIONS

Earflap Border: (Make 2.) With Black and a double-pointed needle cast on 5 stitches using the Two-Strand Cast-On (page 10). Work 8 rows garter stitch (4 ridges on the right side). Work 6 rows each Gray, Burgundy, and Pink (now there should be 13 ridges on the right side). Work 1 row White, then begin working short rows (still using White):

> *K4 , turn and work back.
> K3, turn and work back.
> K2, turn and work back.
> K1, turn and work back.*
> Knit 2 complete rows, 5 stitches for each.
> Repeat short rows, * to *, as above.

Finish bottom of earflap with one complete row of White on the wrong side (the side with the color-change ridges). Work 6 rows each of Pink, Burgundy, Gray. Work 8 rows of Black. Cast off 5 stitches.

Earflap Center: With Black, pick up and knit 28 stitches along inner edge of U-shaped Earflap Border.

> Row 1: With Black k13, k2 tog, k13.
> Row 2: With Gray k12, sl2, k1, p2sso, k12.
> Row 3: With Gray k11, sl2, k1, p2sso, k11.
> Row 4: With Burgundy k10, sl2, k1, p2sso, k10.
> Row 5: With Burgundy K9, sl2, k1, p2sso, K9.
> Row 6: With Pink k8, sl2, k1, p2sso, k8.
> Row 7: With Pink k7, sl2, k1, p2sso, k7.
> Row 8: With White K6, sl2, k1, p2sso, k6.
> Row 9: With White K5, sl2, k1, p2sso, k5.
> Row 10: Bind off in White. Sew the bound-off stitches together.

Repeat with the other earflap.

Begin Body: With Black, cast on 13 stitches using Chain Cast-On (page 9), pick up and knit 21 sts across the top of one earflap, cast on 52, pick up 21 stitches across the other earflap, cast on 13. Join, being careful not to twist. You now have 120 stitches.

> Work Chart A using Black as the MC for the first 2 rounds and Gray as the MC for the last 4. Work one round plain in Gray.
>
> Work Chart B with Gray as MC. Work 1 round plain in Gray.
>
> Work Chart C using Gray as MC for 4 rounds and Black for the final 2.

Shape Crown:

> Round 31: *K5, k2 tog, k6, k2 tog*; repeat around in Black (104 stitches).
>
> Rounds 32–38: Follow Chart D, using Black as MC and using Gray in place of White as CC.
>
> Round 39: With Black *K2, k2 tog, k2, k2 tog, k3, k2 tog*; repeat around (80 stitches).
>
> Rounds 40–43: Work rounds 2–5 of Chart A using the same Black as MC for round 2, Gray as MC for rounds 3–5.
>
> Round 44: With Gray *K1, k2 tog, k2, k2 tog, k1, k2 tog*; repeat around (56 stitches).
>
> Rounds 45–48: Work Chart E with Gray as MC.
>
> Round 49: With Gray *K1, k2 tog, k2, k2 tog*; repeat around (40 stitches).
>
> Round 50: Work Chart F using Gray for MC for first 2 rounds, Black for third round.
>
> Round 53: With Black *K1, k2 tog, k2 tog*; repeat around (24 stitches).
>
> Round 54: Knit around.
>
> Round 55: *K1, k2 tog*; repeat around (8 stitches).

Once finished, break off the yarn with an 8-inch tail and thread the end into a yarn needle. Draw the thread through remaining stitches and fasten off. Using Black, crochet around the cap and earflaps with single crochet.

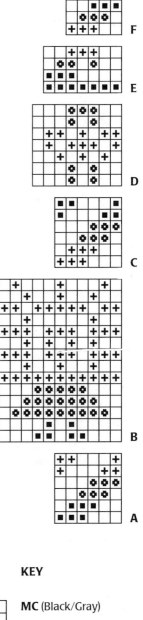

KEY

☐	**MC** (Black/Gray)
■	**Burgundy**
+	**White** (for Chart D only: Gray)
✿	**Pink**

69

Child's Andean Cap

I have intentionally left ties off the earflaps of this cap for safety reasons. (Pictured on page 21.)

For information on converting measurements and yarn weights to metric, see page 88.

SIZE: Small. Cap circumference 16 inches.

YARN: Worsted weight 100% wool, 4-ply, 210 to 220 yds per 3½ oz; 1 skein Gray (Main Color), 1 oz each White and Burgundy.

GAUGE: 6½ stitches and 7½ rows = 1 inch over the pattern.

NEEDLES: Circular needle, 16-in length, and one set of dpn, both size 4, or size needed to knit to gauge, crochet hook size B.
(For equivalent Canadian/ British and metric needle sizes, see page 88.)

INSTRUCTIONS

Earflaps: With Gray cast on 3 stitches using dpn. Work chart in stockinette stitch. Place stitches on a holder. Work the second earflap to match the first.

Begin body: With Gray yarn and circular needle cast on 14 stitches using Chain Cast-On (page 9), knit 19 across the first earflap, cast on 39 stitches for the center front, knit 19 stitches across the second earflap, cast on 14 to complete the back. Join, being careful not to twist. (105 stitches)
Work Chart A. Knit one round using Gray.
Work Chart B. Knit one round in Gray.
Repeat Chart A.

Shape Crown: With Gray work one decrease round as follows: *K6, k2 tog, k5, k2 tog*; repeat around. (91 stitches).
Work Chart C.
With Gray work one decrease round as follows:
K3, k2 tog, k2, k2 tog, k2, k2 tog;
repeat around (70 stitches).
Repeat Chart A. Work decrease round in Gray: *K1, k2 tog, k2 tog*; repeat around (42 stitches).
Work chart D for 5 rounds.
Work decrease round in Gray: *K1, k2 tog*;
repeat around (28 stitches).
K2 tog around (14 stitches).

Break yarn with an 8-inch tail. Thread yarn needle and run through stitches and fasten off.

Scalloped Edge: With crochet hook and Burgundy yarn, starting at the center back, work 3 sc, *ch 3, 3 sc*; repeat around.

EARFLAP

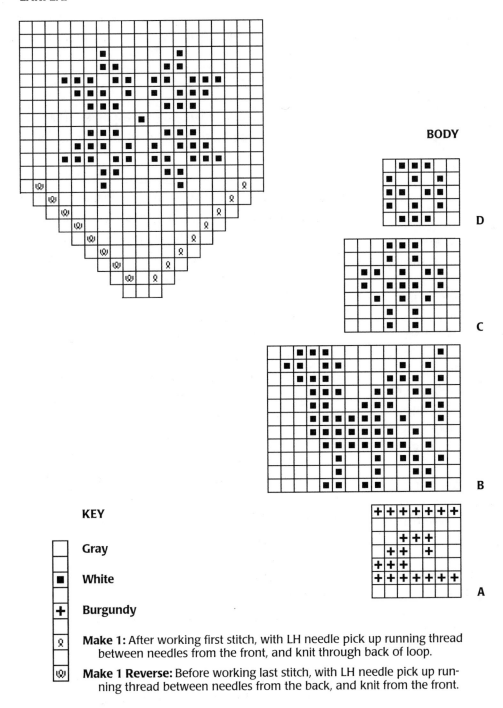

BODY

D

C

B

A

KEY

☐ Gray

■ White

+ Burgundy

Ϙ **Make 1:** After working first stitch, with LH needle pick up running thread between needles from the front, and knit through back of loop.

⋓ **Make 1 Reverse:** Before working last stitch, with LH needle pick up running thread between needles from the back, and knit from the front.

Danish Earflap Cap

This cap uses a two-color pattern from an Old Danish sweater and a fancy Scandinavian-style crown. It is a good warm cap, as it has a double-thickness hem and earflaps—a style I found in a qiviut hat pattern by Kristie Sherrodd in Spin-Off *magazine (Spring 1998, p. 38). (Pictured on page 22.)*

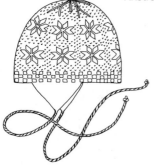

For information on converting measurements and yarn weights to metric, see page 88.

SIZES: Small, (Medium, Large). Cap circumference 16 (18²/₃, 21¹/₃) inches.

YARN: Smooth worsted weight wool, 109 yds per 50 g (1³/₄ oz); 2 skeins Blue (Main Color), 1 skein White (Contrast Color).

GAUGE: 6 stitches and 6 rounds = 1 inch, using larger needles over pattern for body.

NEEDLES: Circular needles, 16-in length, size 4 and size 6, and one set of dpn size 6, or size needed to knit to gauge.
(For equivalent Canadian/ British and metric needle sizes, see page 88.)

INSTRUCTIONS

With larger circular needle and MC cast on 96, (112, 128) stitches using Chain Cast-On (page 9). Join, being careful not to twist.

Hem and Earflaps: Change to smaller circular needle and work in stockinette stitch for 2 inches. Place marker at the beginning of the round. In this round you will begin working short rows, leaving the "dormant" earflap stitches on the circular needle as you proceed:

>P7, (8, 11), k23, (27, 29), turn.
>
>P23, (27, 29), turn.
>
>K22, (26, 28) turn.
>
>P21 (25, 27), turn.
>
>Continue in stockinette, working one less stitch each row until you have worked a row of 4 sts. Turn.

Now reverse the process, picking up "dormant" earflap stitches one at a time along the edges:

>Work 4 sts, turn. Work 5 sts, turn. Work 6 sts, turn. Continue until you have worked a row of 23, (27, 29) sts. One earflap complete.

P33, (39, 45), k23, (27, 29), and work second earflap to correspond with the first. Purl to end of round [10, (11, 14) sts].

Body: Change to larger circular needle. Begin working body chart at round indicated for your size. When you have worked 2 inches of body pattern, pick up the hem into the next row.

Picking Up the Hem: With a double-pointed needle, pick up one stitch along the cast-on edge for every stitch cast on; knit each stitch with its corresponding live stitch, being careful to maintain the pattern of the body of the cap. It may be easier to pick up one stitch at a time rather than picking up a needle full. This method joins the hem invisibly and in an absolutely straight line. (If you prefer, you may sew the hem when the cap is complete. Turn hem at purl bump.)

Crown: Switch to double-pointed needles now, or when there are too few stitches to support the circular needle. Work crown chart for your size (4 repeats each round).

Break off the yarn with an 8-inch tail. Thread tail through remaining stitches and fasten off. Make a 2-color lanyard cord (page 15) for each earflap.

CROWN

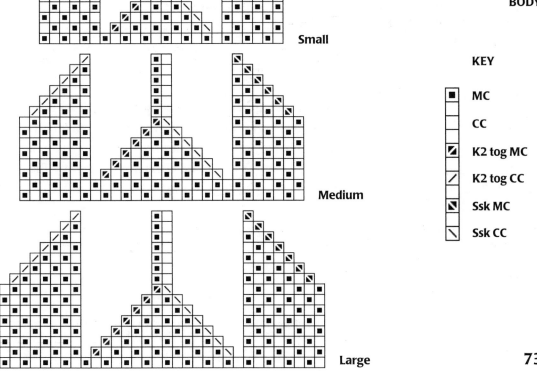

Small

Medium

Large

BODY

KEY

■	MC
☐	CC
◪	K2 tog MC
◢	K2 tog CC
◨	Ssk MC
◺	Ssk CC

Multicolor Whimsical Cap

It is fun to play with textures and colors to create a whimsical cap. The brighter the better! Here is the chance for you to create an outrageous color mix. Each pattern band can be a different color combination, or you can have a theme with a color. (Pictured on page 24.)

For information on converting measurements and yarn weights to metric, see page 88.

SIZE: Adult large.* Cap circumference 20 inches.

YARN: Heavy worsted weight* (85% Wool/15% Mohair, 190 yds per 4 oz, in example shown); 4 ounces total weight.

GAUGE: 4½ stitches = 1 inch over 2-color stockinette stitch.

NEEDLES: Circular needle, 16-in length, and one set of dpn, both size 8, or size needed to knit to gauge. *(For equivalent Canadian/ British and metric needle sizes, see page 88.)*

INSTRUCTIONS

Body: With circular needle cast on 90 stitches using Two-Strand Cast-On (page 10). Join, being careful not to twist. Work 2 ridges of garter stitch (knit one round, purl one round makes one ridge). Work the body chart. Note that each pattern band has a garter-stitch ridge at top and bottom for added textural interest. This ridge is also where you make the color changes. For maximum contrast, it is good to alternate dark and light background colors as you go from one pattern band to the next.

When chart is complete, work 3 rounds of Herringbone:
> Round 1: K1 MC, k1 CC, work around.
> Round 2: Move yarn to the front, p1 MC, set yarn just worked down to the left, bring the other over, p1 CC.
> Round 3: P1 MC, p1 CC, set yarn just worked to the right and bring the yarn to be worked under it.

Crown: Change to MC you are using for the crown pattern and knit one round plain, increasing one stitch in that round. Switch to double-pointed needles now, or when there are too few stitches to support the circular needle. Work the crown chart until there are 7 stitches on the needles.

Break off the yarn with an 8-inch tail and thread the end into a yarn needle. Draw the thread through remaining stitches and fasten off.

*Note that you need to use a heavy worsted weight yarn to match the gauge; a lighter worsted will not produce a distinctive enough texture.

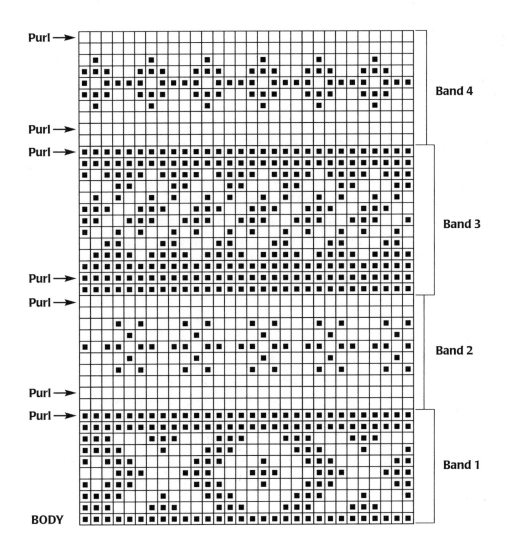

Purl →

Band 4

Purl →
Purl →

Band 3

Purl →
Purl →

Band 2

Purl →
Purl →

Band 1

BODY

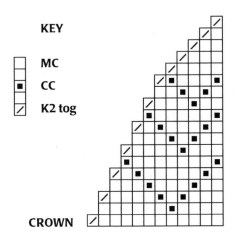

KEY

MC

■ CC

╱ K2 tog

CROWN

To Knit Cap in Other Sizes: I have given instructions for size Large only, as one of the motifs—a favorite of mine—has a repeat of 30 stitches. To make other sizes, substitute a smaller motif taken from a pattern dictionary.

Given this gauge, to make the cap in Small (Medium, X-Large) you would cast on 72 (81, 99) stitches and work the body for a total of 4 (4¾, 6) inches. Then work the herringbone rows and finish with a crown similar to the one I have used.

Jester's Cap

With snowboarding now an Olympic event, there are no limits on winter headwear. The bells will warn those down the hill. (Pictured on page 24.)

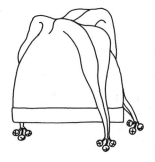

For information on converting measurements and yarn weights to metric, see page 88.

SIZES: Small (Medium, Large, X-Large). Cap circumference 16 (18, 20, 22) inches.

YARN: Worsted weight 100% wool, 4-ply, 210 to 220 yds per 3½ oz; 2 skeins in colors of your choice. (I used 2 similar colors inthe example shown, for a very subtle stripe effect.) Total weight of size Large is 110 grams (approximately 4 oz).

GAUGE: 5½ stitches and 8 rounds = 1 inch.

Specifications continue on next page.

INSTRUCTIONS

With circular needle cast on 90 (100, 110, 120) stitches using Two-Strand Cast-On, Two-Color (page11). Using one needle, cast on with color A over the index finger and Color B over the thumb. After you have cast on the number of stitches required, drop the two slip stitches you used to start the cast-on. Join, being careful not to twist.

A Note about Working One-Round Stripes: With Color B knit the first round. When you have completed the first round, drop Color B and pick up Color A. Work a round and then drop Color A and pick up Color B. By working in this way you will have one-round stripes of two colors without jogs or floats. When you get to the three-pointed crown, continue in this manner but be careful that the color drop is not at the decrease or increase, as you want to be able to keep track of the increasing and decreasing easily.

Cuff and Body: Beginning with Color B, work 1½ inches of k1, p1 ribbing. Change to stockinette stitch, altering the number of stitches as follows in the first round: 0 (-1, +1, 0), for a total of 90 (99, 111, 120) stitches. Work until the piece (including ribbing) measures 4½ (5¼, 6, 6¾) inches, and you have finished working a Color B round.

Shaping the crown: In order to get the three points of the crown to arc out from the center of the cap, there are increases on the outside of the crown and decreases opposite the increases. Double decreases are worked in the even-numbered rounds, and increases are worked every sixth round. Net decrease is 4 stitches over 6 rounds.

Crown Point # 1: Using double-pointed needles and Color A knit the first 15 (17, 19, 20) stitches onto the first needle. Onto the second needle k2 tog, k13 (k16; k18; k2 tog, k18), then cast on to the third needle 14 (16, 18, 20) stitches. Work with the fourth double-pointed needle.

> Preparation Round: Using Color B knit 14 (16, 18, 19), increase two stitches in the last stitch on needle 1 by working k1, yo, k1. Knit across needle 2. On needle 3: K6 (7, 8, 9), k2 tog, k6 (7, 8, 9).
>
> Rounds 1, 3, and 5: Work plain using Color A. When working round 1, move the last stitch from needle 1 onto needle 2. This will keep the increased stitches lined up at the end of needle 1.
>
> Rounds 2 and 4 (double decrease rounds): Use Color B. As you work round 2 *for the first time,* you will establish where the double decreases will be worked on subsequent rounds: k36 (41, 46, 49), then work a double decrease by sl2, k1, p2sso, knit to end of round. For round 4 and all subsequest even-numbered rounds, work to 1 stitch before the previous double decrease, sl2, k1, p2sso, knit to end of round.
>
> Round 6: Using Color B, knit to the last stitch on needle 1 and work a double increase into the last stitch: k1, yo, k1. Knit across needle 2. Needle 3: Knit to one stitch before the previous double decrease, then work the double decrease as established and knit to end of round.
>
> Repeat these 6 rounds until you have 3 stitches left.

As you are working, you need to keep track of where the in-creases and decreases are and line them up. Also, the third needle, where the double decrease takes place, will lose

NEEDLES: Circular needle, 16-in length, and one set of dpn, both size 6, or size needed to knit to gauge. *(For equivalent Canadian/ British and metric needle sizes, see page 88.)*

BELLS: Nine ⅜-inch bells (optional).

stitches. You need to redistribute stitches on the needles from time to time to accommodate the increasing on one side of the crown and decreasing on the other.

Once finished, break off the yarn with a tail about 8 inches long and thread the end into a yarn needle. Draw the thread through the remaining stitches and fasten off.

Crown Point #2: Using double-pointed needles and Color A, knit the first 15 (17, 19, 20) stitches onto the first needle. Onto the second needle k2 tog, k13 (k16; k18; k2 tog, k18). Cast onto the third needle 7 (8, 9, 10) stitches, and then pick up 7 (8, 9, 10) stitches from the base of the first point. Continue as for the first point.

Crown Point #3: Using double-pointed needles and Color A, knit the first 15 (17, 19, 20) stitches onto the first needle. Onto the second needle k2 tog, k13 (k16; k18; k2 tog, k18). Pick up onto the third needle 7 (8, 9, 10) stitches from the base of one point, and then pick up 7 (8, 9, 10) stitches from the base of the other completed point. Continue as for the first point.

Finishing: Attach 3 bells to each point. (You may substitute a tassel or small pom-pom.)

Brimmed Cap

Many brimmed caps are now felted. Felting can be tricky, though; I've seen some that didn't felt and others that felted too much. If you match the gauge, you know what you're getting with this pattern. Although this cap is not actually felted, it is knit at a gauge that produces a tight, dense fabric, making it as warm as a felted cap. A fluffier "woolen"-spun yarn makes a denser fabric than a smoother worsted-spun yarn does. (Pictured on page 20.)

INSTRUCTIONS

With circular needle cast on 117 (135, 144, 162) stitches using Two-Strand Cast-On (page 10). Join, being careful not to twist.

Brim: Knit two rounds. Increase to 130 (150, 160, 180) stitches: *k9, inc1*, repeat around. Work 1 1/3 (1 1/2, 1 3/4, 2) inches. Decrease to 117 (135, 144, 162) stitches: *k8, k2 tog,* repeat around. Knit for 3/4 (1, 1 1/4, 1 1/3) inches. Decrease to 91 (105, 112, 126) stitches: *k3, k2 tog, k2, k2 tog,* repeat around.

Body: Work for 3 1/2 (4, 4 2/3, 5 1/3) inches.

Crown: Adjust to 90 (102, 108, 120) stitches by decreasing 1 (3, 4, 0) stitches in the next round evenly. Switch to double-pointed needles now, or when there are too few stitches to support the circular needle.

> Next round: *K13 (15, 16, 18), k2 tog, place marker* repeat around.
> Each subsequent round: Knit until there are 2 stitches before the marker, k2 tog. Continue until there are 6 stitches left on the needle.

Break off the yarn with an 8-inch tail and thread the end into a yarn needle. Draw the thread through remaining stitches and fasten off.

For information on converting measurements and yarn weights to metric, see page 88.

SIZES: Small (Medium, Large, X-Large). Cap circumference 16 (18, 20, 22) inches.

YARN: Worsted weight, 100% wool, 210 yards per 4 oz; 1 skein.

GAUGE: 5 3/4 stitches = 1 inch.

NEEDLES: Circular needle, 16-in length, and one set of dpn, both size 4, or size needed to knit to gauge. *(For equivalent Canadian/ British and metric needle sizes, see page 88.)*

Topflappen Cap

Topflappen is translated literally as "pot holder," from German. It is great fun to work with these small squares and put the cap all together without sewing, using only two double-pointed needles. The squares are from Horst Schultz's book, Das Neue Stricken Kindermode. *(Pictured on page 17.)*

For information on converting measurements and yarn weights to metric, see page 88.

SIZE: Adult Large. Cap circumference 19½ inches.

YARN: Worsted weight, 85% Wool/15% Mohair, 190 yds per 4 oz; 1 skein of Black (MC) and a few ounces each of 5 contrast colors (CC). You may use more than 5 colors. Each square uses only a few yards.

GAUGE: Square measured on the diagonal: 3¼ inches.

NEEDLES: Circular needle, 16-in length, and one set of dpn, both size 6, or size needed to knit to gauge. *(For equivalent Canadian/ British and metric needle sizes, see page 88.)*

INSTRUCTIONS

This cap is created by knitting a series of small squares and half squares. The body of the cap is worked from the top down. Then stitches are picked up along the lower edge to knit the cuff. The crown is finished last.

Half Squares:
> Row 1: Using MC, cast on 22 stitches using Chain Cast-On (page 9)
> Row 2: K2 tog tbl, k8, k2 tog, k9, sl1 wyif.
> Row 3: Change to CC. K2 tog tbl, k7, k3 tog, k7, sl1 wyif.
> Row 4: K2 tog tbl, p14, sl1 wyif.
> Row 5: With MC, K2 tog tbl, k5, k3 tog, k5, sl1 wyif.
> Row 6: K2 tog tbl, k10, sl1 wyif.
> Row 7: With CC, K2 tog tbl, k3, k3 tog, k3, sl1 wyif.
> Row 8: K2 tog tbl, p6, sl1 wyif.
> Row 9: With MC, K2 tog tbl, k1, k3 tog, k1, sl1 wyif.
> Row 10: Bind off.

Full Squares: With MC pick up 22 stitches (11 from the right-hand square and 11 from the left-hand square, weaving in the tail end as you go.) Turn.
> Row 2: Knit 10, k2 tog, k9, slip last stitch wyif.
> Row 3: With CC, k9, k3 tog, k8, slip last stitch wyif.
> Row 4: K1, purl to the last stitch, slip last stitch wyif.
> Row 5: With MC, k8, k3 tog, k7, slip last stitch wyif.
> Row 6: Knit to the last stitch, slip the last stitch wyif.
> Row 7: With CC, k7, k3 tog, k6, slip last stitch wyif.
> Row 8: K1, purl to the last stitch slip last stitch wyif.

Continue working CC and MC rows as established, decreasing with a k3 tog in the center of each right-side row.

Remember that the first stitch of every row is knit and the last stitch of every row is slipped with the yarn in front. This slipped stitch gives an even edge and is useful for picking up stitches later.

Row 21 (last row): With MC, k3 tog. Fasten off.

Working in the ends: Since each square is knit with 2 colors of yarn, there are two ends to deal with. The easiest way to clean up the ends is to weave them under the working yarn when knitting the first row with that yarn: hold the end above and then under the working yarn until it is all caught under the stitches of the worked row. You can also do this with the cut tail from a previous square. This will eliminate having to sew in these ends when the cap is complete.

Body: Start by making 6 half squares. Place 2 half squares together with their "peaks" pointing up. With MC, pick up 11 stitches starting from the peak of the right-hand half square and working down to the base. Then pick up 11 more stitches working up to the peak of the left-hand half square. Complete the full square as described above. (The directions for full squares begin with Row 2 because you will have already worked Row 1 as you picked up your 22 starting stitches.)

When you get to full square #6, you will be closing the circle of the cap. Continue working more full squares, using the colors in random fashion, picking up stitches along the sides of squares already worked. After you have completed full square 18, make a final round of half squares.

Cuff: Using MC pick up and knit 78 stitches along the edge of the series of half squares that you just finished (13 stitches across the long side of each half square).

Round 2: Purl.
Rounds 3 and 4: Knit CC.
Round 5: Knit MC.

Round 6: Purl MC.

Rounds 7 and 8: Knit CC.

Round 9: Knit MC.

Round 10: Purl MC.

Bind off in MC.

Crown: Using MC, beginning at the center of one of the half squares, pick up and knit 90 stitches (15 stitches for each half square). Switch to double-pointed needles now, or when there are too few stitches to support the circular needle.

Round 2: MC *p6, p3 tog, p6*; repeat around.

Round 3: CC knit around.

Round 4: CC *k5, k3 tog, k5*; repeat around.

Round 5: MC knit around.

Round 6: MC *p4, p3 tog, p4*; repeat around.

Round 7: CC knit around.

Round 8: CC *k3, k3 tog, k3*; repeat around.

Round 9: MC knit around.

Round10: MC *p2, p3 tog, p2*; repeat around.

Round 11: C knit around.

Round 12: CC *k1, k3 tog, k1*; repeat around.

Round 13: MC knit around.

Round 14: MC *k3 tog*; repeat around.

Break off the yarn with an 8-inch tail and thread the end into a yarn needle. Draw the thread through remaining stitches and fasten off.

Bavarian Tree Ornament

Bavarian patterns are similar to Aran patterns; however, the German patterns utilize twisted-knit stitches, which make the patterns more distinct. (Pictured on page 24.)

INSTRUCTIONS

Cuff: With MC cast on 48 stitches using Chain Cast-On (page 9). Divide onto 3 needles: 16 stitches on the first needle, 14 on the second, 18 on the third—this arrangement will make it easier to work the twisted stitches. Join, being careful not to twist. Work 5 rounds k1b, p1 rib.

Body: Work the Bavarian pattern (see detailed directions below) until the whole piece measures 1 1/2 inches.

Crown: Work the next 4 rounds as k2 tog, decreasing the number of stitches from 48 to 24, then 12, then 6, and then 3. Using those 3 stitches, work about 3 inches of I-cord and fasten the end of the I-cord to the top of the cap to create a loop for hanging.

I-Cord: Knit the 3 stitches as usual. Do not turn the work, but slide the 3 stitches to the other end of the needle and knit them again. Be sure to pull the yarn tight on the first stitch. You are creating a small tube of circular knitting. K3 tog to finish the I-cord.

BAVARIAN PATTERN

Twisted Knit: Every knit stitch is twisted, i.e., knit through the back of the loop. When the instructions say k2b, it means that you knit both stitches through the back of the loop.

RTKP: With both stitches on the LH needle—a purl and a knit—insert the right needle in the back of the knit stitch (the second stitch) and knit the stitch through the back of the loop but do not slip the worked stitch off the LH needle yet. Slip the first (purl) stitch to the RH needle, slip the worked stitch off the LH needle, then slip the purl stitch back to the LH needle and purl that stitch.

For information on converting measurements and yarn weights to metric, see page 88.

SIZE: About 1 1/2 inches from cuff to top of crown.

YARN: Fingering weight yarn—about 10 yds.

GAUGE: 10 stitches = 1 inch.

NEEDLES: One set of dpn size 0, or size you feel comfortable using. *(For equivalent Canadian/ British and metric needle sizes, see page 88.)*

RT: With both stitches on the LH needle—twisted-knit stitches—insert the right needle in the back of the *second* stitch on the needle and knit the stitch through the back of the loop but do not slip the worked stitch off the LH needle yet. Slip the *first* stitch to the RH needle, slip the worked stitch off the LH needle, then slip the first stitch back to the LH needle and knit that stitch through the back of the loop.

Round 1: P2, k2b, p2, k1b, p3, k2b; repeat around.

Round 2: P2, RT, p2, k1b, p2, RTKP, k1b; repeat around.

Round 3: P2, k2b, p2, k1b, p1, RTKP, p1, k1b; repeat around.

Round 4: P2, RT, p2, k1b, RTKP, p2, k1b; repeat around.

Round 5: P2, k2b, p2, k2b, p3, k1b; repeat around.

Round 6: P2, RT, p2, k1b, p3, k2b; repeat around.

Round 7: P2, k2b, p2, k1b, p2, RTKP, k1b; repeat around.

Round 8: P2, RT, p2, k1b, p1, RTKP, p1, k1b; repeat around.

Round 9: P2, k2b, p2, k1b, RTKP, p2, k1b; repeat around.

Round 10: P2, RT, p2, k2b, p3, k1b; repeat around.

Two-Color Christmas Ornament

I found these such fun to knit that I thought I'd never go back to full-sized caps. They also make great decorations for gifts. (Pictured on page 24.)

INSTRUCTIONS

Body: With MC cast on 48 stitches using Chain Cast-On (page 9), divide onto 3 needles (16 stitches on each). Join, being careful not to twist. Work the chart through round 9.

At Round 10 you will join the hem to the body of the cap as follows: With another double-pointed needle pick up 1 stitch along cast-on edge for every stitch cast on; knit each stitch with its corresponding live stitch on the left-hand needle. (It is easiest to pick up 1 stitch at a time and knit it with its corresponding live stitch before moving on to the next stitch.) Continue working to the top of the chart.

Crown: Change to working with MC only (and work in the loose end of CC as you proceed). Work the next 4 rounds as k2 tog. The number of stitches will thus decrease from 48 to 24, then 12, then 6, and then 3. On those 3 stitches work about 3 inches of I-cord.

I-Cord: Knit the 3 stitches as usual. Do not turn the work, but slide the 3 stitches to the other end of the needle and knit them again. Be sure to pull the yarn tight on the first stitch. You are creating a small tube of circular knitting. K3 tog to finish the I-cord, then fasten the end of the cord at the top of the cap to create a loop for hanging.

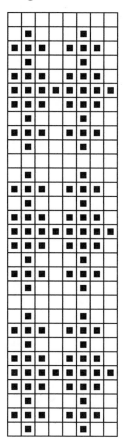

For information on converting measurements and yarn weights to metric, see page 88.

SIZE: About 1 1/2 inches from cuff to top of crown.

YARN: Fingering weight yarn—a few yds each of two colors, Dark CC and Light MC.

GAUGE: 10 stitches = 1 inch.

NEEDLES: One set of dpn size 0, or size needed to knit to gauge.
(For equivalent Canadian/ British and metric needle sizes, see page 88.)

KEY

☐	MC
■	CC

USEFUL THINGS TO KNOW

ABBREVIATIONS USED IN THE CAP PATTERNS

dpn: double-pointed needle

k2 tog: Knit 2 stitches together through front of loops as one stitch.

k1b: Knit one stitch in back loop.

sl2, k1, psso: Insert needle into the second and first stitches as if to k2 tog, and slip both stitches at once from this position; knit next stitch, then pass the 2 slipped stitches together over the knit stitch.

sl1, k2 tog, psso: Slip 1 st with yarn in back, knit next 2 sts together, then pass the slipped stitch over the knit stitch.

ssk: (Slip, slip, knit.) Slip the first and second stitches one at a time as if to knit, then insert point of left-hand needle into the fronts of these 2 stitches and knit them together from this position.

tbl: Through the back of the loop.

wyif: With the yarn in front of the slipped stitch.

make 1 (M1): Insert left needle, from front to back, under strand between last stitch knitted and next st, and pick up onto left needle. Knit into the loop at the back of the needle, twisting the strand as you do so.

yarn over (yo): Take the yarn over the top of the needle once before making the next stitch. On the next round the stitch is worked as a single stitch.

EQUIVALENT NEEDLE SIZES

Note that sizes do not always correspond exactly between one measurement system and another.

USA	Can./U.K.	Metric (mm)
0	14	2
1	13	2.25
-	-	2.5
2	12	2.75
-	11	3
3	10	3.25
4	-	3.5
5	9	3.75
-	8	4
6	-	4.25
7	7	4.5
8	6	5

Circular needles: 16-inch = 40cm; 24-inch = 60cm.

CONVERSIONS FOR METRIC MEASUREMENTS

To convert inches to centimeters, multiply by 2.54. In the following list, measurements have been rounded to the nearest 0.25cm.

½ inch	1.25cm
¾ inch	2cm
1 inch	2.5cm
2 inches	5cm
3 inches	7.5cm
4 inches	10cm
5 inches	12.5cm
6 inches	15.25cm
7 inches	17.75cm
8 inches	20cm
9 inches	22.75cm
10 inches	25.25cm

To convert yards to meters, multiply by 0.91. A skein of 220 yards = 200 meters.

To convert ounces to grams, multiply by 28.35. A 3½-ounce skein = 100 grams.